LIBRARY FUNDING
AND
PUBLIC
SUPPORT

A Working Paper on the Background

and Issues

by

ROBERT W. FRASE

with testimony by
EILEEN D. COOKE
and other source documents

AMERICAN LIBRARY ASSOCIATION
Chicago 1973

Library of Congress Cataloging in Publication Data

Frase, Robert William, 1912-
    Library funding and public support.

    1. Libraries and state--United States.
2. Federal aid to libraries--United States.
I. American Library Association. II. Title.
Z678.F75   021.8'3'0973   73-17396
ISBN 0-8389-3150-2

Printed in the United States of America

CONTENTS

TABLES

INTRODUCTION

On June 8, 1973, a group of citizens experienced in the field of communications met in New York to discuss their concern about access by the American public to books and journals through organized collections in libraries. At issue was the impact of a change in public policy on library support and the crisis presented by proposed termination of $176 million in federal library funding for college, school, and public libraries. Robert W. Frase, formerly economist for the Association of American Publishers, presented to the group a background paper, which, with slight revisions incorporating developments up to September 1, 1973, is the major text of this publication. The Frase report, together with the accompanying source documents, attest to the need for continued support of national library policy and programs.

That group of concerned citizens—speaking as individuals but expressing representative views from their respective fields of library, book, and journal communications systems—regarded the Administration's budget proposal for abandoning federal support for libraries as a serious step backward, one which would severely and immediately damage the national interest. They issued a statement, appended herein as the second source document, urging the President and the U.S. Senate to avoid a reversal of established federal government policy of support for a national library system.

In testimony, on May 17, 1973, Eileen D. Cooke, director of the American Library Association's Washington Office, presented the position of the American Library Association at the hearings before a subcommittee of the Committee on Appropriations of the House of Representatives. Her testimony is appended as the first source document.

Other documents appended are the ALA resolution adopted by the Council of the American Library Association at the Association's Midwinter meeting in January 1973, and the Memorandum of Resolution voted by the Board of Directors of the Association of American University Presses on June 19, 1973.

The major events in the federal appropriations process in the period June-August inclusive were in the passage by the House of Representatives of the FY 1974 Labor-HEW Appropriations Bill (HR 8877) on June 26,

1973, and Presidential signature on July 1, on a "continuing resolution" for the period July 1–September 30. The significance of these actions and an analysis of the future outlook is shown in the following remarks of Mr. Frase, excerpted from his follow-up article, "Federal Library Funding Cuts—How Will They Affect the Book Market?" *(Publishers Weekly, September 3, 1973, p. 22)*:

The final answer to whether the Administration will succeed in eliminating federal library programs or whether the Congress will prevail in continuing to fund these programs is not likely to be given until October or November at the earliest, and perhaps several months later if it goes into the courts.

The appropriations situation in the 1974 fiscal year is extraordinarily complex, but the main elements can be summarized readily enough. The House of Representatives has passed the Labor-HEW 1974 Appropriations Bill, which carries funding for the three major library programs at approximately the 1972 level. . . .

The Senate is not scheduled to act on the 1974 Appropriations Bill until mid- or late September, but is expected to appropriate at least as much as the House for library programs. However, the entire Labor-HEW Appropriations Bill, which may exceed the President's budget by a billion dollars or more, may well be vetoed and the two-thirds vote in both Houses of Congress necessary to override a Presidential veto may not be there. If a veto is not overridden, the Congress may bring out a substitute Labor-HEW Appropriations Bill with lower amounts, and this substitute bill in turn may or may not be vetoed. Last year two consecutive Labor-HEW Appropriation Bills were successfully vetoed and library program funding was based on a "continuing resolution," under which the Administration spent not at the levels directed by the Congress but at the levels in the President's budget. This reduced spending at the budget level under the continuing resolution was not as serious last year for library programs as it would be this year because in 1973 the library programs were not at a zero level in the budget.

This year there is also a continuing resolution applicable until September 30, 1973, which directs library program spending at the level of the House-passed bill . . . .

The Administration has not as yet released any library program money under the continuing resolution and is not expected to do so until one of two things happens: (1) the President signs a Labor-HEW Appropriations Bill, or (2) the courts order the funds to be spent under a continuing resolution.

Several suits which were brought around the country in the spring of 1973 resulted in various district court judges ordering the release of appropriated but unspent funds, including library program funds, appropriated by the 1973 continuing resolution. The Administration has released some of these funds under the district court orders, but has continued to withhold other funds ordered to be spent by the district courts. The Administration is also appealing some of these district court orders to spend impounded funds. It can be expected that if the Administration refrains from spending education and library funds appropriated for fiscal 1974 under a new regular appropriations bill or a continuing resolution, various states will file to force spending.

In late August, the Administration announced interim provisions for continuing the library programs in fiscal year 1974. According to this revised plan, the Library Services and Construction Act will be funded at the annual rate of $13 million; Title II of the Elementary and Secondary Education Act at the annual rate of $14.5 million.

An even more determined return to the established federal government policy of support for a national library system is needed. This publication is offered in response to a call for "such action as may be necessary to create a full public awareness of the scope and severity of the problems we confront."

September 12, 1973

BOOKS, JOURNALS, AND LIBRARIES AS A SYSTEM OF COMMUNICATION AND ITS RELATIONSHIP TO OTHER COMMUNICATIONS MEDIA: Three Earlier Studies

There has been a great deal of writing about communications media in the last thirty or forty years, but it is fragmented and has many gaps. Only a small part is of direct relevance to the subject matter of this conference. Much of the professional literature, both in articles and books, deals with the various aspects of individual communications media such as newspapers, magazines, radio, and television. Another whole body of literature is written from the point of view of a particular intellectual discipline such as the law or sociology. This is true of both individual scholarly efforts and of foundation and government supported major research undertakings. Relatively little has been done to consider the whole range of the communications media, to analyze the particular strengths and functions of each, especially as related to their economic bases, and to go on to consideration of public policy problems.

THE LACK OF ECONOMIC ANALYSIS

One of the reasons for the unsatisfactory state of broad and critical analyses of communications policy is the lack of economic studies. Economic factors such as the market and cost are one of the fundamental determinants of the content as well as the availability of the media. Wilbur Schramm, director of the Institute of Communications Research at Stanford University, had this to say in the second edition of his book of readings on *Mass Communications* (Univ. of Illinois Press, 1960):

> There is no satisfactory book on the economics of mass communication. A few articles appeared in the journals about ten years ago, but unfortunately the data in most of those articles are now outdated. The FCC provides a certain amount of economic data on broadcasting, and the trade press frequently carries current data. Such sources as these, an occasional article, a few pamphlets issued by the industry, a publishing house, newspaper chain, or network, is what we shall have to depend on until a definite book is written.

The situation which Dr. Schramm describes is still largely true in 1973, both in general and with respect to the individual communications media. This generalization can be illustrated in that portion of the communications structure with which this conference is concerned. The only two full-length books which deal with the book industry and its economics are O.H. Cheney's *Economic Survey of the Book Industry 1930-31* (Bowker reprint edition, 1960) and William Miller's *The Book Industry* (Columbia Univ. Press, 1949, part of the Public Library Inquiry). In addition to being outdated, neither of these books was written by an economist and neither dealt with the whole range of book publishing and distribution. Robert W. Frase did the first analysis of economics of publishing and distribution of general books and its effect on content in a Windsor lecture at the University of Illinois in 1952, published in *Books and the Mass Market* (Univ. of Illinois Press, 1953) which was supplemented by occasional short articles in professional journals in subsequent years. Theodore B. Peterson in his book *Magazines in the Twentieth Century* (Univ. of Illinois Press, 1956), and earlier in journal articles, had analyzed the fundamental economic structure of that part of magazine publishing dependent on advertising and its influence on content. Not until 1968 was there a beginning of economic analysis of library service in a group of studies prepared under contract for the National Advisory Commission on Libraries by Professor William J. Baumol and others, published in part in *Libraries At Large* (Bowker, 1969).

LACY's *Freedom and Communications*

Building on the methods of economic analysis developed by Frase and Peterson and drawing on his experience at the Library of Congress and the American Book Publishers Council, Dan Lacy broke new ground in his three Windsor Lectures published in 1961 under the title *Freedom and Communications* (Univ. of Illinois Press). These lectures are so central to our subject matter that arrangements have been made to supply copies of the paperback edition to the conference participants rather than to attempt to paraphrase or reproduce lengthy portions in this paper. The three most important contributions to our conference subject matter in the Lacy work, largely in chapters 2 and 3, are:

1. The treatment of books, journals, and libraries as part of an interrelated single system of communications
2. An analysis of this system of communication, especially its economic basis, as compared with other systems such as radio, television, the newspaper press, and large circulation periodicals
3. Some examination of the impact of public policy on all the major systems of communications, including the book-journal-library complex.

REPORT OF THE NATIONAL
ADVISORY COMMISSION ON LIBRARIES

The report and papers of the National Advisory Commission on Libraries

(1966-68) are also relevant to the subject matter of this conference. These documents represent the only recent effort to analyze and assess the functions of libraries of all types. Although the report itself and the commission's studies represent a valuable contribution to the subject matter of this conference, the commission for the most part did not deal with any but the most general public policy issues. The objectives set for the commission in President Lyndon B. Johnson's executive order of September 2, 1966, were to:

1. Make a comprehensive study and appraisal of the role of libraries as resources for scholarly pursuits, as centers for the dissemination of knowledge, and as components of the evolving national information systems
2. Appraise the policies, programs, and practices of public agencies and private institutions and organizations, together with other factors, which have a bearing on the role and effective utilization of libraries
3. Appraise library funding, including federal support of libraries, to determine how funds available for the construction and support of libraries and library services can be more effectively and efficiently utilized
4. Develop recommendations for action by government or private institutions and organizations, designed to ensure an effective and efficient library system for the nation.

The recommendations of the Advisory Commission are touched upon again later in this paper in the chapter on public support of libraries. However, a number of points may be briefly noted here:

1. The Advisory Commission found that library service was of sufficient general interest to require the adoption of a national policy on libraries and therefore recommended the adoption of the following statement:

> RECOMMENDATION: That it be declared National Policy, enunciated by the President and enacted into law by the Congress, that the American people should be provided with library and informational services adequate to their needs, and that the Federal Government, in collaboration with state and local governments and private agencies, should exercise leadership in assuring the provision of such services.

2. To implement this National Policy on Libraries the Commission recommended the "establishment of a National Commission on Libraries and Information Science as a continuing federal planning agency."

3. Both of these recommendations were accepted by the Congress and approved by the President in Public Law 91-345 of July 20, 1970, an act establishing a permanent National Commission on Libraries and Information Science. The statement of policy in the Congressional act was slightly different in wording but not in substance from that recommended by the Advisory Commission and read as follows:

> Sec. 2. The Congress hereby affirms that library and information services adequate to meet the needs of the people of the United States are essential to achieve national goals and to utilize most effectively the Nation's educa-

tional resources and that the Federal Government will cooperate with State and local governments and public and private agencies in assuring optimum provision of such services.

4. Members of the Commission were not appointed until May, 1971. Because of delay in providing appropriations the Commission did not begin to meet until September 1971, and an executive director was not appointed until January, 1972.

5. The inquiries of the National Advisory Commission on Libraries and its report and recommendations, no doubt because of the limitations in the specific wording in President Johnson's charge, were directly and rather exclusively to the problems of libraries and library systems narrowly conceived. The commission did not deal with the other half of the system of communications which is the focus of this conference—the creation of materials, principally books and pamphlets—which libraries help to make available to the public but also organize in such a way as to make the whole far more than the sum of the parts.

The Production and Distribution of Knowledge in the United States

Mention also needs to be made of the study by Professor Fritz Machlup published as *The Production and Distribution of Knowledge in the United States* (Princeton Univ. Press, 1962). This is a largely factual and statistical study of the "knowledge industries" including education, research and development, media of communication, information machines, and information services. (Libraries are mentioned only briefly in connection with education.) Professor Machlup treats information and knowledge as synonymous and includes in his economic measurements of the knowledge industries all the participants, from the actual creators to the most routine disseminators. He does not deal with public policy questions.

Professor Machlup's study is of interest to our concerns in placing the communications media in a much broader setting of development and dissemination of knowledge. Of particular interest to us in considering the special role of the book-journal-library complex in the whole gamut of communications is his effort to estimate the nature of types of knowledge conveyed by the various communications media. Professor Machlup's classification of types of knowledge is as follows:

Using then the subject meaning of the known to the knower as the criterion, I propose to distinguish five types of knowledge:

1) Practical knowledge: useful in his work, his decisions, and actions; can be subdivided, according to his activities, into
    (a) Professional knowledge
    (b) Business knowledge
    (c) Workman's knowledge

(d) Political knowledge

(e) Household knowledge

(f) Other practical knowledge

2) Intellectual knowledge: satisfying his intellectual curiosity, regarded as part of liberal education, humanistic and scientific learning, general culture; acquired, as a rule, in active concentration with an appreciation of the existence of open problems and cultural values.

3) Small-talk and pastime knowledge: satisfying the nonintellectual curiosity or his desire for light entertainment and emotional stimulation, including local gossip, news of crimes and accidents, light novels, stories, jokes, games, etc.; acquired, as a rule, in passive relaxation from "serious" pursuits; apt to dull his sensitiveness.

4) Spiritual knowledge: related to his religious knowledge of God and of the ways to the salvation of the soul.

5) Unwanted knowledge: outside his interests, usually accidentally acquired, aimlessly retained.

The results of Professor Machlup's attempts at measurement are shown in table 1, assembled from various parts of chapter 6 of his book.

Each of these estimates was made on the basis of certain arbitrary assumptions using available statistics and tabulations by other authors. No two methods are identical. Advertising space is not counted in this case of newspapers and is shown separately in the case of radio and television networks.

TABLE 1
TYPES OF KNOWLEDGE CONVEYED BY VARIOUS MEDIA
OF COMMUNICATION
(IN PERCENTAGES)

MEDIUM	PRACTI-CAL	INTEL-LEC-TUAL	PAS-TIME	SPIRI-TUAL	ADVER-TISING	MISC.
Books (titles) 1958	15.6	50.6	24.1	7.8	—	1.9
Books (copies) 1958	39.9	37.7	15.7	6.7	—	—
Periodicals (receipts) 1954	35.3	22.4	36.5	5.8	—	—
Newspapers (space) 1954	7.9	33.4	51.4	2.0	—	5.3
Phonograph records (titles) 1961	—	23.0	77.0	—	—	—
Motion pictures (not analyzed)	—	—	—	—	—	—
Radio (time) 1957	10.5	12.0	65.6	4.4	7.5	—
Television networks (time) 1960	—	9.8	75.2	—	15.0	—
Libraries (not analyzed)	—	—	—	—	—	—

SOURCE: Fritz Machlup, *The Production and Distribution of Knowledge in the United States.* (Princeton Univ. Press, 1962), Chap. 6.

CHAPTER 2

PUBLIC
SUPPORT OF LIBRARIES

One of the most important issues of public policy in the long run—and by far the most pressing in the short run—is whether there should be a national policy and a national program relating to library service. Up until January, 1973, there had been a gradual development of a consensus over a period of years that a national policy was required and that the federal government should resume responsibility for coordinating the continuing development of that policy as well as shouldering a considerable share of the financial burden. The Congress had enacted the National Commission on Libraries and Information Science Act, and the President had appointed the commission in May, 1971. The commission was charged with the following responsibilities:

Sec. 5. (a) The Commission shall have the primary responsibility for developing or recommending overall plans for, and advising the appropriate governments and agencies on, the policy set forth in section 2. In carrying out that responsibility, the Commission shall—

(1) advise the President and the Congress on the implementation of national policy by such statements, presentations, and reports as it deems appropriate;

(2) conduct studies, surveys, and analyses of the library and informational needs of the Nation, including the special library and informational needs of rural areas and of economically, socially, or culturally deprived persons, and the means by which these needs may be met through information centers, through the libraries of elementary and secondary schools and institutions of higher education, and through public, research, special, and other types of libraries;

(3) appraise the adequacies and deficiencies of current library and information resources and services and evaluate the effectiveness of current library and information science programs;

(4) develop overall plans for meeting national library and informational needs and for the coordination of activities at the Federal, State, and local levels, taking into consideration all of the library and informational resources of the Nation to meet those needs;

(5) be authorized to advise Federal, State, local, and private agencies regarding library and information sciences;

(6) promote research and development activities which will extend and improve the Nation's library and information-handling capability as essential links in the national communications networks.

In addition, the federal government had, beginning in 1956, gradually taken on responsibility for substantial programs of financial assistance for the support and systematic development of the public library system, library training and research, school libraries, and college and university libraries. Although there was disagreement beginning in 1969 between the Congress and the Administration on the appropriate level of funding for these programs, the Administration as late as 1972 had recommended in its budget for the federal fiscal year 1973 a total of $140 million for these library programs.

This gradual development and implementation of a national library policy was abruptly reversed when the Administration budget of the fiscal year ending June 30, 1974, was presented to the Congress in January, 1973, without prior consultation with the National Commission on Libraries. The 1974 budget recommended no funds whatsoever, even of a transitional or terminating nature, for all of the library programs.

Table 2 shows the major federal library programs; the amounts of federal expenditures in the fiscal year ending June 30, 1972; the amounts of appropriations by the Congress for the 1973 fiscal year; the recommendations in the President's budget for fiscal year 1974; and the amounts passed by the House of Representatives in the Labor-HEW 1971 Appropriations Bill. Also included in the table are two other programs relating to audio-visual materials and equipment; the first for elementary and secondary education (about 20 percent for materials and 80 percent for equipment) and the second for colleges (about 50 percent for materials).

As the figures in table 2 indicate, there was a drastic change in federal policy recommended by the Administration between its budget submissions on library programs for the fiscal years 1973 and 1974. What are the reasons given for this abrupt change in policy? This is not very clear, but for the public library program and the school library program, general revenue sharing and educational revenue sharing were held out as alternative sources of federal funds. With respect to the college library materials program, the detailed budget documents submitted to the Congress merely stated:

> Federal support of higher education is shifting from categorical institutional assistance toward student assistance. Federal assistance to higher education will be concentrated on students who will carry the funds to the institutions of their choice.

Revenue Sharing a Substitute?

Thus in two cases revenue sharing is held out as a substitute source of federal funds. As a practical matter, however, this is not a realistic alterna-

TABLE 2

FISCAL 1972-74 APPROPRIATIONS FOR MAJOR LIBRARY PROGRAMS
(IN MILLIONS OF DOLLARS)

PROGRAM	1972 CONGRESSIONAL APPROPRIATIONS	1973 PRESIDENT'S BUDGET	1973 CONGRESSIONAL APPROPRIATIONS	1973 RELEASED BY PRESIDENT	1974 PRESIDENT'S BUDGET	1974 HOUSE BILL HR 8877
Public Library Services (LSCA I and III)	$ 49.2	$ 32.7	$ 69.5	$ 32.7	0	$ 49.2*
Public Library Construction (LSCA II)	9.5	0	15.0	0	0	9.5
School Library Resources (ESEA II)	90.0	90.0	100.0	90.0	0	90.0
College Library Resources (HEA II)	11.0	12.5	12.5	12.5	0	10.5
Library Training and Research (HEA II)	4.7	5.3	5.3	5.3	0	4.5
Subtotal	$164.4	$140.5	$202.3	$140.5	0	$163.7
Equipment, Materials, and Minor Remodeling (NDEA III)	50.0	0	Up to 50.0	2.0	0	25.0
Undergraduate Instructional Materials and Equipment (HEA VI)	12.5	0	Up to 12.5	0	0	12.5
Total	$226.9	$140.5	$264.8	$142.5	0	$201.2

NOTE: In a letter to Chairman Magnuson of the Senate Appropriations Subcommittee on Labor-HEW dated August 9, 1973, Secretary of HEW Casper Weinberger urged that the budget total of the 1974 bill be held, but agreed to accept some House cuts in certain programs and to increase the amount in the budget for certain other programs. All of these changes were in nominal amounts. For example, Weinberger proposed to raise the figure for the Library Services Program from zero to $13.0 million, and for the School Library Program from zero to $14.5 million. The college library materials program was still recommended for elimination in this latest Weinberger proposal.

*Figures are also the annual spending levels authorized in the "continuing resolution," Public Law 93-52, for the period July 1-September 30, 1973.

tive especially for the short run in the fiscal year 1974. Public libraries are eligible for allocations of funds by state and local governments under the General Revenue Sharing Act passed in 1972. However, public libraries must compete with demands for funds for other eligible purposes such as pollution control and law enforcement as well as the use of federal revenue sharing funds for local property tax reductions. Further, unlike the LSCA requirements for matching and "floor" level expenditures, general revenue sharing funds may be, and are being, used to substitute for funds previously available from state and local sources. An abrupt shift of this kind, from ongoing operations financed over a period of years by a specialized federal grant-in-aid program based on state plans to alternate sources of financing, primarily locally, cannot in fact be made. The practical result, if the Administration recommendation to provide no funds in fiscal year 1974 for the Library Services and Construction Act is adopted, will be a massive disruption of public library service. Data collected in May show that if no federal public library funds are available in fiscal year 1974, over 2,300 staff members in public libraries will have lost their jobs as of July 1, 1973. Other public library personnel now employed and paid by federal funds will be kept on the job by diverting local and state funds from other budget categories, principally funds intended for the purchase of new and replacement materials, mostly books and magazines.

As of early May, 1973, reports on federal revenue sharing in the first fiscal year of that program indicated that public library service projects totaling $10,575,035 had received, or had been promised, funding with the state or local share of federal revenue sharing money. This compares with $49.2 million of federal money appropriated by the Congress for public library services in the fiscal year 1972. Some 97 percent of revenue sharing monies were local funds and therefore for strictly local projects rather than regional, statewide, and other projects designed to provide systematic library coverage of entire states. Thus revenue sharing was not showing much prospect of taking up the slack if Library Service Act appropriations for library service were abruptly terminated in fiscal 1974. On library construction the picture was different: $21.8 million under revenue sharing in fiscal 1973 as compared with $9.5 million under LSCA in 1972.

SCHOOL LIBRARIES

In the case of the school library program (Title II ESEA), the possibility of shifting to a new source of federal financing is even more remote in the short run. Administration witnesses from the Department of Health, Education and Welfare and the Office of Education made their first presentations of a special Education Revenue Sharing Bill ("Better Schools Act of 1973") before a House Committee on March 19, 1973, and before a Senate Subcommittee on April 9. Members of both parties on the Senate and House appropriations and education committees have already indicated that the drastic shift therein proposed, to an entirely new pattern of federal aid to elementary and secondary education, cannot possibly be enacted by the Congress in time to form the funding basis for the 1974 fiscal year beginning July 1, 1973—funding which is needed by the educational systems for the academic year beginning September, 1973. The Congress will, of necessity, be forced to appropriate on the basis of the programs authorized by existing law. If the Administration does not accept this alternative, it could lead to the veto of education and library appropriations voted by the Congress and/or the President's impounding or withholding of funds for the school library program as well as other programs authorized by the present Elementary and Secondary Education Act.

Even in the longer run, the Administration proposal for school library programs in the special Education Revenue Sharing bill presents great uncertainties. The school library materials program is proposed to be carried out—at the discretion of the states and of local school systems— from a combined fund of $420 million proposed for fiscal year 1975 allocated for one or more of some fourteen present separate programs, among them being school library resources, school pupil personnel services, adult education, and school meals. The total dollar amount for all states is only about two-thirds of the well over $600 million which was made available for the same purposes in the fiscal year 1973. In addition, the Administration draft bill for special education revenue sharing (introduced by request in the House by Congressman Bell of California as H.R. 5823 and in the Senate by Senator Dominick as S. 1319) would permit the unlimited transfer of these general support funds from the specified purposes enumerated above, including school libraries, to the following different purposes: disadvantaged and handicapped children and vocational education. Thus in practice under the Administration's proposed bill, a local school district could elect to spend no funds whatsoever for school libraries. This would amount to the abandonment of a policy of ensuring that all elementary and secondary schools have adequate libraries, at a time when about one-third of all elementary schools still have no libraries at all.

College Libraries

In the case of the college library materials program, the Administration budget for fiscal 1974 proposes termination with no substitute in new legislation. Thus, colleges and universities which will receive in fiscal 1973 some $12.5 million in federal funds for materials acquisitions—which constitute almost 5 percent of their total acquisition funds—will either have to find money for this purpose elsewhere or cut back on acquisitions. In view of the general financial crisis in higher education, the latter alternative is not a realistic prospect. The reduction in these acquisitions will have a variety of impacts on academic programs which cannot function effectively without current library resources, especially in new and growing institu-

14

tions. New and recently established junior and community colleges, for example, already face a double burden: they must not only acquire the current output of books, periodicals, and other library materials, but they must make up the accumulated backlog of older materials which are essential if these institutions are to provide quality education.

SUPPORT OF DIRECT FEDERAL LIBRARY PROGRAMS

It should be noted that the recommended elimination of federal grant-in-aid programs for libraries in the 1974 budget has not been accompanied by similar treatment of important nationwide library functions carried out by the three national libraries: the Library of Congress, the National Library of Medicine, and the National Agricultural Library.

The Library of Congress is a special case because as part of the legislative branch of the government it is not subject to the normal executive branch budget process. In addition to its service to the Congress it performs important functions for the entire library system of the country in cataloging of domestic and foreign works, sale of cataloging information on catalog cards and MARC tapes, acquisition of foreign materials, and compilation of union catalogs. In fact, rather than being cut back, the library has secured approval of the House Appropriations Committee to expand its regular budget in 1974 to finance a major new program of incorporating cataloging information in U.S. books (Cataloging in Publication) which was started with the aid of foundation funds.

The National Library of Medicine and the National Agricultural Library perform many of the same services for the library system of the country as the Library of Congress in their subject matter fields: medicine and related sciences and agriculture and related sciences. Their funds, which are carried in the HEW and Agriculture Appropriations Bills respectively, are recommended in the 1974 budget at about the same level as the previous year.

The National Commission on Libraries and Information Science, which has an authorized spending level of up to $750,000 in its basic act, received only $200,000 in 1972 and 1973, and appears in the HEW budget for fiscal 1974 at $406,000.

THE INFLUENCE OF LIBRARIES ON PUBLISHING

Sales to libraries have a direct influence on what is published and what is kept in print, and therefore on what is available for purchase and use by individuals and institutions both at home and abroad. The discussion of this relationship will be confined to book publishing, for which sufficient statistical and other data exist to make meaningful analysis possible. Unfortunately, this is not the case for journals, but no doubt many of the same relationships obtain in that area, especially for small and specialized journals.

15

What proportions of all sales of books in the United States are made to libraries? This can be estimated with a good deal of accuracy by one method, and checked by another.

In the latest year for which data are available, the calendar year 1972, the total revenue of publishers (including exports of all books as well as overseas sales of encyclopedias by American companies publishing abroad) came to a total of $3.2 billion.

Sales to libraries cannot as yet be counted directly because the large volume of book sales to libraries which go through wholesalers cannot be traced. Thus, it is necessary to start at the other end with data on library expenditures. Relatively hard figures are available for academic libraries (college and university) and for public libraries from the inquiries into library budgets by the Bowker Company. The figures are for the year 1972–73, and are based on very comprehensive surveys. Unfortunately, no data are available for school libraries in any recent year, but we do know that the federal government alone has been making grants to local school districts for the purchase of school library materials in the last two years at the rate of $90 million annually, of which about $50 million was used for books. A figure of three times this amount seems a reasonable estimate of total book expenditures to those familiar with the field, and is consistent with some partial data available from federal program reports. In comparing library purchases of books with publishers' sales data, adjustments have to be made for the charges made by wholesalers and for library purchases of foreign books not distributed in the United States by American publishers. The necessary adjustments are shown in table 3:

If we approach the equation from the other direction, drawing upon judgments in the trade as to the percentage of sales to libraries for the several types of books, we come up with much the same total of library sales. Table 4 shows these estimates and calculations.

It will be noted in table 4 that some types of books are particularly dependent upon library sales. The two leading categories are hard-bound original editions of children's books and university press books. The same would be true of certain portions of other categories of nonfiction in which the editions are small and the library portion of sales very high. A substantial reduction in library sales is thus certain to make many hundreds of potential titles uneconomic, even for partially subsidized works published by nonprofit organizations such as university presses. The total of library sales compared to all book sales looks rather small—about 12 percent—but when one eliminates the types of books that are not at all dependent on the library market, or only to an insignificant extent, total domestic book sales are only about $950 million. Academic, public, and school library sales of $384 million account for 40 percent of that figure. Since established libraries tend to buy a higher proportion of newly published books than of books published in

TABLE 3

ESTIMATED 1972-73 LIBRARY BOOK PURCHASES
(IN MILLIONS OF DOLLARS)

	TOTAL BOOK PURCHASES	LESS FOREIGN PORTION	DOMESTIC BOOK PURCHASES	LESS WHOLE-SALER CHARGES	NET REVENUE TO PUB-LISHERS
Academic libraries	$184	—15%	$156	—5%	$148
Public libraries	139	—5%	132	—15%	111
School libraries	150	—2%	147	—15%	125
Total	$473		$435		$384

TABLE 4

ESTIMATED PORTION OF PUBLISHERS' 1972 SALES TO
ACADEMIC, PUBLIC, AND SCHOOL LIBRARIES
(IN MILLIONS OF DOLLARS)

TYPES OF BOOKS (U.S. CENSUS CATEGORIES)	PUBLISHERS' REVENUES	PERCENTAGE LIBRARY SALES	ESTIMATED LIBRARY SALES
Adult trade			
Hardbound	$ 243	35	$ 85
Paperbound	55	20	11
Juvenile books			
Retail: under $1.00	24	10	3
Retail: $1.00 and over	128	80	102
Bibles, testaments, hymnals, and prayer books	63	—	—
Other religious books	63	20	13
Professional books			
Law	94	20	19
Medicine	65	30	19
Business	41	30	12
Technical, scientific, and vocational	150	20	30
Book clubs	304	2	6
Wholesaled (mass-market) paperbound	253	5	13
University press	41	45	18
Elementary and secondary textbooks	498	—	—
College textbooks	375	4	15
Standardized tests	27	—	—
Subscription reference books	606	3	18
Other books	147	15	22
Total	$3,177		$386

SOURCE: Publishers' revenues are the estimates contained in the 1972 Association of American Publishers Industry Statistics.

previous years (which represent about half of publishers' total sales in the categories under consideration), the impact of library sales on the publishing of new titles is even greater than this 40 percent figure would suggest.

Federally Funded Portion of Library Book Purchases

The last step in this statistical exercise is to estimate the portion of academic, public, and school library book purchases which have recently been funded from federal appropriations for the major library programs now budgeted for termination. The amounts appropriated and spent in the fiscal year 1972 are used because, while 1973 appropriations by the Congress were higher, substantial withholdings were made by the Administration. Table 5 makes use of estimates compiled by the U.S. Office of Education:

TABLE 5

Money Spent on Books from the Three Major
Federal Library Grant Programs
(In Millions of Dollars)

Public libraries (LSCA, including matching funds)	$ 41
School libraries (ESEA II)	48
College libraries (HEA IIA)	11
Total	$100

This figure of $100 million of federally funded library book acquisitions does not take into account the secondary effects of termination of federal library grant programs, especially the Library Services Act, such as the continuation of formerly federally supported personnel on the payroll but financed by local funds originally budgeted for the acquisition of materials. But even $100 million is over 20 percent of total book expenditures of the three major types of libraries, and the proportion is a third for school libraries and about 30 percent for public libraries. There can be no doubt, therefore, that the abrupt termination of the three major federal grant-in-aid library programs would result not only in a serious deterioration of the quality of library service, but also substantially reduce the publication of important new book titles which appear in small editions and are heavily dependent upon the library market.

CHAPTER 3

POSTAL RATES
AND THE DISTRIBUTION
OF PUBLISHED MATERIALS

In 1970, the United States entered an entirely new era with respect to its postal service. With the passage of the Postal Reorganization Act of 1970, the former Post Office Department was transformed into an independent government corporation—the United States Postal Service. The setting of wage and salary rates for postal employees, which had been a matter of Congressional legislation, became a collective bargaining function between the Postal Service and postal employee unions. The establishment of postal rates for the various classes and subclasses of mail was also relinquished by the Congress and turned over to a Postal Rate Commission appointed by the President.

In July, 1971, the first two-year contract with postal employees came into operation, with substantial increases in wages. In July, 1972, a new schedule of postal rates became effective, with sharply increased rates projected over a five-year period for some types of mail, and over a ten-year period for other types. These five– and ten–year periods of transition or adjustment were mandated by the Reorganization Act, reflecting some appreciation by the Congress that considerably higher rates could be expected. During these five– and ten–year transition periods, the act authorized annual appropriations by the Congress to make up the difference between the revenues from rates and postal service costs. In addition, a general transitional subsidy was authorized for ten years starting with a sum of $920 million and tapering off to zero in the eleventh year.

PAST PREFERENTIAL RATES ON PUBLICATIONS

Although there were other policy issues presented by the reorganization bill, the most important such issue faced by the Congress involved the role of postal service in the dissemination of published materials. For over a century it had been the national policy to provide especially favorable rates to newspapers and magazines (second class matter) on the theory that the encouragement of these publications was in the national interest. These publications provided the information and opinion necessary to the citizen in carrying out his responsibilities in a democracy, and were also a principal vehicle for the nationwide dissemination of scientific, technical, educational, and cultural materials. The rate structure for the second class mail category reflected this philosophy: rates on the editorial content of newspapers and magazines were set particularly low and were uniform for the entire country at a flat rate per pound while rates for advertising material were not only higher but were graduated upward with distance.

Until 1938, books were not included in this deliberate policy of providing favorable rates to published materials, although books served substantially similar purposes as newspapers and magazines and were also heavily dependent on the postal service for distribution, not only to individual consumers but to book stores, schools, colleges, and libraries. In 1938 President Roosevelt, under temporary emergency powers granted him during the depression, established a new and separate nationwide book rate at the same flat rate of 1½ cents per pound which was then applicable to the editorial content of second class newspapers and magazines. Beginning in 1942, this nationwide book rate was continued by acts of Congress, but at a higher level than the rates for second class newspapers and with a higher rate for the first pound than for succeeding pounds. In the late 1950s, this book rate was expanded to include various other educational and cultural materials such as printed music, educational tests, audiovisual materials, and recordings. It came to be known as the "educational rate" or the "special fourth class rate."

These preferential rates for newspapers and magazines and for books undoubtedly required some subsidy of public funds, and this subsidy was clearly recognized and considered as justified by many presidents and many Congresses. The extent of this subsidy was, however, a matter on which opinions differed. If one considered that the Post Office Department existed primarily to transport letters (first class mail) it could be, and was, argued that the general overhead of the post office (representing about half of the total cost) should be carried entirely by first class rates and that auxiliary services such as the distribution of newspapers, magazines, and books should be charged only with the additional cost directly attributable to these auxiliary services. On this basis newspapers and magazines were provided with a relatively modest subsidy, and books none at all. On the other hand, if the general overhead of the post office was charged pro rata to auxiliary services such as the distribution of newspapers, magazines, and books, the subsidies for newspapers and magazines were large and for books substantial.

The Congress had before it in 1970 a variety of proposals for dealing with the policy question of how postal rates for published materials should be set. One proposal, for example, was that for certain of these rates recognized to have public interest components, including those on educational matter, the Congress itself should continue to legislate the level of rates and appropriate subsidies if such rates were set at levels below cost. This view did not prevail and as the act was finally passed, this policy question of setting rates for published materials was left for the most part to the five-man Postal Rate Commission appointed by the President but not subject to Senate confirmation. Only a limited number of policy questions were settled in the legislation itself rather than being left to the discretion of the Rate Commission. For example, certain rates for nonprofit organizations, including the rates on their publications, were not required to share any overhead costs and were to be increased over a ten-year period rather than the normal five; and rates for first class matter and rates on educational and library materials could not be zoned by distance. The general rates for newspapers and magazines (regular second class) and for books and other educational and cultural materials (special fourth class) were included in the general category of rates to be set by the Postal Rate Commission at a level which at least covered directly attributable cost plus such part of the overhead cost as the Commission decided was appropriate. Certain standards were provided in the statute to guide the Commission in the all-important question as to how much of the overhead should be assigned to the various classes and subclasses of mail. These standards, however, were of such a general nature that they did not inhibit the Commission very much in making these policy decisions.

It should be noted that in considering the Postal Reorganization Act in 1969 and 1970, the Congress did not have before it any detailed estimates of future costs, or any guide to the magnitude of rate increases which would result in making the postal services essentially a self-supporting operation over a ten-year period. It seems fair to say that the Congress did not anticipate rate increases of the magnitude which developed out of the first proceeding before the Rate Commission. In introducing a bill on March 28, 1973, to moderate the rate increases scheduled for published materials, Senator Humphrey of Minnesota, a former member of the Post Office Committee, reflected the view of many Senators when he said in looking back to 1970:

> Many Members of the Senate were concerned in 1970 about what would happen to the distribution of informational, educational, and cultural materials through the mails under the Postal Reorganization Act. However, there was no indication 3 years ago that the rate increases under the new system would be of such incredible magnitudes. For example, in the Senate Committee report on the reorganization bill the following passage occurs as an illustration of rate increases which the committee thought might be expected under the new legislation.
>
> Notwithstanding its rejection of a proposal to impose its views on the new Postal Service by law, the committee agreed that this report should specifically express committee concern over the rates to be established for certain classes of mail. Accordingly the committee alerts the Rate Commission established by this bill to the public service which certain preferred rates have historically performed.
>
> Reduced rates for within-county newspapers, for libraries, for books, and for associations of rural electrification co-ops were enacted for very good reason—that the public generally benefits from such rates. Additionally, the

Rate Commission should take into account the preferential rates for the mailings of authorized non-profit organizations . . . ; and the rates of classroom publications. . . .

The committee does not believe that small incremental increases in rates spread out over 5 and 10 year periods will be detrimental to mail matter allowed preferential rates because they contribute to the public welfare. But the Rate Commission should be aware of this special problem as it assembles its schedules of rates and fees.

Despite this assurance, there was enough uneasiness in the Senate on the potential impact of the legislation on the distribution of these materials that the Senate by unanimous vote agreed to a floor amendment by the majority and minority leaders, Mr. MANSFIELD and Mr. SCOTT. This amendment, now in the law, requires that the rates on books, educational films, and other materials in the so-called special fourth-class rate and the library rate be uniform for the entire country. As the sponsors of the amendment stated, the amendment at least guaranteed equal access by the American public to these materials regardless of how far they might live from publishing centers, largely in the East.

We now have had enough experience with postal operations under the reorganization act to realize that the Congress must face once more, in the light of present facts, its responsibilities relating to the impact of increased postal rates on the educational, scientific, cultural, and political life of this country.

Not only did the Congress and its post office committees in 1970 not have before them any realistic projections of future rates from the Post Office Department, but several of the important groups and firms concerned with published materials did not fill this gap with their own projections of cost and rates. Certain associations of magazine publishers actually supported the Postal Reorganization Act on the grounds that service would greatly improve and increases in efficiency would hold down costs and rates. (The library and book associations on the other hand did raise warning signals about the effect of the bill on the distribution of published materials.) In the Senate, the bill which emerged out of the Post Office Committee was not even subject to the normal process of open public hearings and debate on a bill or bills, but was developed entirely *in camera* and subject to discussion for the first time on the Senate floor.

THE COMMISSION RATE INCREASES

Some six months after the passage of the Postal Reorganization Act in the summer of 1970, a very elaborate proceeding to establish new rate schedules was commenced before the newly created Postal Rate Commission. This proceeding began in February, 1971, and was concluded in June, 1972. The postal service proposed a schedule of rates, and by and large this schedule, with relatively minor variations, was approved by the Postal Rate Commission and subsequently ratified by the Board of Gov-

ernors of the Postal Service to take effect on July 6, 1972. The rates
established for regular second class mail (newspapers and magazines) provided for a 126 percent increase evenly spaced in annual increments over
five years and a 70 percent increase was scheduled for special fourth class
mail (books and other educational materials) over the same period. Regular
second class was assigned a share of general postal service overhead in a
sum amounting to 29 percent of the actual cost attributable to that class
of mail. Books were assigned an overhead of roughly twice as much pro-
portionately or 57 percent of the attributable cost. The so-called library
rate (interlibrary loan rate) was increased by 129 percent, stretched out
over a ten-year phasing period, and in accordance with the Postal Reorganization Act, not burdened with any institutional or overhead costs
of the postal service.

The Impact of Postal Rate Increases
on Magazines

Congress had under serious consideration several bills which would
amend the basic Postal Reorganization Act to moderate the rate increases
scheduled for publications in the current five-year period and the even
higher rates which can reasonably be anticipated long before the five-year
period is over. Hearings on these bills before the House Post Office and
Civil Service Committee were completed on March 23, 1972, and before
the parallel Senate Committee on April 3. On July 23, 1973, the House of
Representatives voted down giving any consideration to a bill—H.R. 8929,
the Educational and Cultural Postal Amendments of 1973—which had
been reported out by the House Committee on Post Office and Civil Service. The bill would have extended the phasing period for the initial increases
in rates on magazines and newspapers and on books from five years to
nine years; reduced by one-third presently scheduled rates on commercial newspapers and magazines on the first 100,000 copies and for
nonprofit newspapers and magazines on the first 250,000 copies; confined any future increases in nonprofit newspaper and magazine rates to
one-half of any increases recommended by the Postal Rate Commission;
and required the Postal Rate Commission to take into account in setting
rates the "educational, cultural, scientific, and informational value of mail."
Several bills pending in the Senate incorporated one or more features of the
bill not accepted by the House of Representatives.

The impact of the presently scheduled increases in rates, and the certainty of even higher future rates, promises to be very serious for magazines
commercially published. Newspapers would also be affected, but to a much
lesser degree. Most large city and suburban newspaper circulation is not
dependent on the postal service, but small city and country papers do have
large mail circulations. (Magazines and journals published by nonprofit
organizations enjoy a different rate and will be discussed separately.)

In the magazine field, however, the postal service is the predominant method of distribution. The data for 1971 compiled for the Magazine Publishers' Association for about two-thirds of the total commercially published magazine volume shows the following percentage of revenue by sources for 485 magazines:

From advertising	63.2%
From subscriptions	29.3%
From single copy (news stand) sales	7.5%

The magazine industry has produced a great deal of economic data to back up its claim that unless relief legislation is passed, the presently scheduled and reasonably anticipated second class rates will in all likelihood result in greatly curtailed magazine circulation, discontinuance of magazines, and in the discouragement of new magazines. No industry-wide data are as yet available beyond 1971, and thus the impact of the 30 percent increase in regular second class rates instituted July 6, 1973, cannot yet be precisely measured. However, even before this increase the general economic and competitive situation—especially the impact of television in a time of mounting costs—had resulted in decreases for magazines in the MPA survey from 1966 to 1971 of the following amounts:

In total advertising lineage	5.5%
In advertising pages sold	9.3%

In addition, from 1970 to 1971 there occurred the first actual decrease in the number of copies of magazines distributed by mail—almost 100 million copies—or 5 percent.

Profits after taxes for this large group of magazines had declined from $38 million in 1966 to $14.5 million in 1971, and amounted in 1971 to only 1.6 percent of gross revenues as compared with 4.6 percent in 1966. This percentage of net profit is about the lowest of any manufacturing industry. Projected second class postal rate increases in each of the next four years beginning July 6, 1973, will be higher in each year than the 1971 level of net profits.

In the pre-television age, the increase in second class postage projected over the next four years in the present rate schedule would have presented less of a crisis for magazines. Subscription rates and advertising rates would probably have resulted in some shift of advertising to large newspapers and also to direct mail, both less affected by increased postal costs. However, the major advertising competition is now television (and in prospect CATV) which are not affected by postal costs.

Magazine advertising rates are based upon circulation and television rates on the number of viewers. Even before the beginning of this period of sharply rising postal rates magazines were falling behind in the advertising competition with television. Between 1963 and 1971, nighttime network television advertising base rates increased by 37 percent, but since the

24

viewing audience was rapidly expanding this resulted in only a 5 percent increase in the rate per thousand viewers (CPM). Consumer magazines on the other hand raised their base rates by 25 percent during the same period, which resulted in a CPM increase of 7.5 percent or half again as much as network television rates.

The Magazine Publishers' Association commissioned an economic study by R.J. Barbour assessing the possibility of still further increases in second class postal rates in the next four years beyond those in the present schedule. Barbour's estimates were based on the assumptions that the total costs of the postal service (which are 85 percent personnel costs) would increase for the next four years at the rate of 10 percent a year, which was the average increase in the three-year period 1968-1971. On this basis, and assuming that the Postal Rate Commission will continue to assign the same proportion of overhead to second class rates, the projected rate increases for the five-year period, 1972-1977, would be to a level of 406 percent over 1971. This would result in a $5–a–year second class postage increase for a typical weekly magazine.

Even if one assumes a lesser increase in postal cost for the next four years than Barbour's 10 percent, it is clear that postal rates will have a serious effect on magazine distribution. Just to break even, magazine subscription prices and advertising rates would need to be substantially increased. With each increase in subscription prices some decrease in circulation will certainly occur, which in turn will still further increase advertising rates based on cost per thousand (CPM). Competition from other advertising media, especially television, will hold down the possible advertising rate increases without losing advertising business. The prospects are that existing magazines will go out of existence, others will shift to a concentration on higher income consumers, editorial cost will be trimmed, and the entry of new magazines will be discouraged.

What are the public policy issues presented by this prospect? Magazines will come to play less of a role as a source of information, opinion, and culture, and the role of alternative means of communication will increase. This means primarily television, newspapers, and books at the present time, with cable television of potential major importance in the not-too-distant future. The nature of television programming and newspaper content is not likely to change much. Both are essential for current news, and a good many newspapers also provide more extended analysis as well as day-by-day commentary in their editorial pages and syndicated columns. However, magazines are a more suitable vehicle for extended analysis and commentary and also cover a much broader range of subject matter and spectrum of opinion than broadcast television or newspapers. Books could take up some of the slack. They are better suited than magazines to extended analysis and cover an even wider spectrum of opinion. In a limited number of cases they can also be produced quickly and widely distributed. Examples are the paperback editions of such works as the *Warren Commission*

Report and the *Pentagon Papers*. The amount of substitution by other media will, however, be limited. With a shrinkage in the magazine field, there can be little doubt that we shall be less well informed as citizens and have reduced access to a wide range of opinion, information, and scientific, economic, and cultural material.

The question thus presents itself as to how much it would cost in public funds to prevent this deterioration in the magazine field. Before examining this question, however, let us first look at the situation with respect to nonprofit magazines and the prospect for books under projected and prospective rate increases, and then undertake the arithmetic for both magazines and books.

NONPROFIT MAGAZINES

The Postal Reorganization Act provides separate and more favorable treatment on rates for nonprofit newspapers, magazines, and journals—those published by nonprofit organizations serving educational, scientific, religious, charitable, and similar purposes—than for commercially published newspapers and magazines, and for all books (whether published by commercial firms or nonprofit organizations). These so-called nonprofit publications enjoy two advantages:

1. The rates applicable to them are not required to bear any of the overhead costs of the Postal Service
2. Increases in their rates are required to be stretched out over a five-year rather than a ten-year transitional period.

Thus, nonprofit second class publications will enjoy substantially lower rates than commercial publications not only for the next nine years during the balance of the transitional period, but indefinitely after that time under the present language of the Postal Reorganization Act. The volume of these publications moving through the postal system is very substantial—some 2.2 billion pieces a year, roughly two-fifths of the volume of commercial second class publications. A large part of the whole body of scientific and professional journals with which this conference is concerned and which form such an important part of organized collections of libraries is eligible for this special preferential rate.

THE IMPACT ON BOOK PUBLISHING
AND DISTRIBUTION

The economics of postal costs in the publication and distribution of books is quite different than from magazines. In the first place, books carry no advertising, and in fact under the postal statutes cannot carry advertising (except for incidental announcements of other books) and qualify for the special fourth class rate. This means that the entire income must come from the sale of books themselves plus secondary rights such as paperback and book club publication, translations, dramatization, television, and motion picture rights. Thus, the important calculation for magazines of advertising income based on circulation volume does not enter into the determination of whether a book is economically feasible. Secondly, for the most part postage costs on books are paid directly by the recipient (whether individual, consumer, book store, school, or library), and are not part of the cost of doing business for the publisher. The economic impact of higher postage charges comes about through its effect on the consumer demand for books.

The postal service is the single most important distribution vehicle for books—as it is for magazines—but the proportion of total sales distributed through the mails is not quite as high. Table 6 shows expert judgments concerning the relative use of the postal service in the distribution of various types of books presented in the first postal rate case in 1971:

About 50 percent of shipments of books to schools, higher education institutions, libraries and colleges are by mail.

TABLE 6

USE OF THE POSTAL SERVICE IN DISTRIBUTION
OF VARIOUS TYPES OF BOOKS

USE AND CATEGORY	PERCENTAGE BY MAIL
HEAVY USE	
Encyclopedias and other subscription reference books	Close to 100
Annual supplements to encyclopedias	100
Teachers' examination copies of textbooks	Close to 100
University press books	Close to 100
Shipments to college and university libraries	50 to 100
Shipments to small public and school libraries	Close to 100
Book clubs	Close to 100
Books sold by direct mail	100
MEDIUM USE	
College textbooks	About 50
Shipments to bookstores outside large metropolitan areas	At least 50
Shipments to public libraries outside metropolitan areas	At least 50
LIGHT USE	
Elementary and secondary textbooks	Most shipments by truck except for emergency and supplementary supplies
Mass market paperbacks	The vast majority by truck to the local magazine wholesalers who do local distribution

Table 7 shows the level of rates for books and other special fourth class materials in 1971 (the last rate established by the Congress) and the schedule of rates of 1972-77 which resulted from the first postal rate decision in 1972.

TABLE 7

LEVEL OF RATES FOR BOOKS AND OTHER SPECIAL FOURTH CLASS MATERIALS
SCHEDULE OF RATES

LEVELS	1971*	1972–73	1973–74	1974–75	1975–76	1976–77
First pound	12	14	16	17	19	21
Succeeding pound	6	7	8	8	9	10
Percentage increase over 1971†	0	17	33	40	50	70

NOTE: The years shown are from July 6 through July 5.

*These were the last rates established by the U.S. Congress.

†Percentage increases must be based on an assumption as to the relative proportion of first pounds and succeeding pounds. The percentages shown for some intermediate years are based on the proportions used by the U.S. Postal Service for 1972.

TABLE 8

SPECIAL FOURTH CLASS RATE COSTS
(IN MILLIONS OF DOLLARS)

	1971	1972–73	1973–74	1974–75	1975–76	1976–77
Revenues	$96.6	—	—	—	—	$306.8
Percentage increases over 1971	0	17	33*	—	—	314

*Assuming no increase beyond presently scheduled rates in 1973-74, because a new postal rate proceeding before the Commission would take time, and a new rate schedule might not take effect before July 6, 1974.

If the same assumptions used by R. J. Barbour in projecting increased postal costs for 1977 for regular second class are accepted, the result would be still greater increases in costs and overhead assigned to the special fourth class rate as shown in Table 8.

Thus, on these assumptions, the book rate would need to be increased by 314 percent over the 1971 level: to approximately 38 cents for the first pound and 19 cents for succeeding pounds or 57 cents for the usual single book package, compared with the 18 cents in 1971.

Increases of this magnitude would have a depressing effect on the consumption of books generally, but a disproportionate impact will be on institutional purchases by schools and libraries of all types. Representatives of the American Library Association testified both in the 1971-72 postal rate case and before Congressional Committees in 1972 and 1973 that increases in postage charges on library purchases of books would come out of library book budgets and the result would be a dollar reduction in book purchases for each dollar of the increased postage cost. Taken together with the financial crisis faced by libraries and the threatened removal of all federal financial support for libraries discussed earlier, these postal increases would still further reduce the ability of libraries to keep up with necessary current additions of materials with which they perform their function of serving the public.

COSTS OF RELIEF

We turn now to the costs of the relief provided in the bills before the Congress. The form of relief in these bills which is most likely to be accepted by the Congress and is also the easiest to calculate is the extension of the five-year transitional period to ten years. The U.S. Postal Service has estimated in a report to the House Committee that the cost of this extension for regular rate second class matter over a nine-year period would total $345 million, or an average of about $39 million per year. For books and other special fourth class materials the equivalent figure would be $129 million over nine years or an average of about $14 million per year. These sums compare with total annual postal costs in 1972 of $9.5 billion. As the bills are now drafted these sums would be provided in additional transitional appropriations by the Congress.

The second provision in the amending bills most likely to be accepted by the Congress is the addition of the requirement that the Postal Rate Commission take into account in setting rates the "educational, cultural, and scientific value to the recipient of mailed materials," which the Commission has thus far been reluctant to do. The impact of such a requirement is hard to estimate, but it could significantly reduce the magnitude of future rate increases on newspapers, magazines, and books, while very slightly raising future increases on other classes of mail, such as first class parcel post and direct mail advertising matter.

POSTAL RECLASSIFICATION—A POTENTIAL HAZARD

The matter of postal "reclassification" needs also to be mentioned, although at this time developments in this area are difficult to predict. Mail classes and subclasses have developed historically over a long period of time and contain a number of anomalies and inconsistencies. In the Postal Reorganization Act, the Congress gave the Postal Rate Commission the power—after formal proceedings—to recommend changes in the classification system which would go into effect with the force of law if approved by the Board of Governors of the Postal Service. Such a classification proceeding before the Commission is just getting under way, and the postal service has recommended some relatively minor changes and refinements in the present system, leaving the basic structure untouched. The Postal Rate Commission on the other hand has indicated clearly that it wishes to consider much more radical and sweeping changes.

29

The basic reason for the modest reclassification proposals of the Postal Service are the legal requirements in the Postal Reorganization Act that various classes and subclasses of mail be provided with five– and ten–year transition periods to higher rates, which is incompatible with a drastic change in the system of classification. In addition, with respect to certain materials, such as books, included in the present special fourth class and library interchange rates, the statute also guarantees nationwide flat rates not zoned by distance. This also inhibits classification changes.

Nonetheless, if the Postal Rate Commission persists in trying to bring about radical classification changes, a danger would arise that scientific, educational, and cultural products might be lumped together with other materials strictly on the basis of their physical characteristics as packages in the mail stream, to the further deterioration of their treatment in the postal system, both as to rates and quality and speed of service.

CHAPTER 4

BOOKS, JOURNALS, AND LIBRARIES
AS PART OF THE INTERNATIONAL
NETWORK OF COMMUNICATIONS

The principal media or systems of communication have for centuries extended across national boundaries, some more than others, but almost all of them to a very much greater extent in the last three decades. Newspapers, television, and radio are served by worldwide press services. Many newspapers and some magazines and broadcast networks have their own foreign correspondents. A few magazines have large foreign editions in several languages. Popular music, especially American, has a worldwide audience.

Books, journals, and libraries are no exception to this general development. In fact, this may be the most international of the systems of communication. A very high proportion of the audience this system serves is made up of the intellectual, scientific, cultural, political, and economic elite in developed and developing countries alike; and these elites are habitually more concerned with new developments wherever they may occur than the general population.

Prior to World War II, the United States was a net importer of intellectual and cultural products. This was reflected among other things in an import balance on books and scientific and professional journals. Since 1945, the situation has turned around. We are now the world's greatest exporter of books and journals as well as one of the very largest importers. Many of our scientific, technical, and professional journals have 25 to 50 percent of their sale abroad. A number of interrelated developments have contributed to this change, including massive amounts of money invested in research and development and higher education, and the exploitation of the initial advantage of English as the language most common in the developed countries of the world. Our libraries, especially large research and academic libraries, working both individually and cooperatively among themselves and with the Library of Congress, have become among the strongest in the world in the international scope of their collections.

This trend toward increased internationalization of the book-journal-library complex since the end of World War II has been accompanied by parallel changes in U.S. government policy. Since 1954, the United States has for the first time joined an international copyright convention, eliminated its import tariffs on books, music, and a variety of other educational, cultural, and scientific materials, and adopted a preferential schedule of international postal rates on publications and music. No one of these specific changes came about automatically. Each one of them was the result of hard, long, and persistent work by a few civil servants working with book, library, and associated organizations over a period of years. On the other hand, without the fact, the climate and the economic reality of increased internationalization, these changes in government policy could not have occurred.

By and large the present status of public policy on international issues relating to the book-journal-library system is a good one. As already indicated, several of the essential steps necessary to promoting the free international flow of educational, scientific, and cultural materials have been taken and embodied in rather long-lasting institutional and legal commitments. But there are improvements still to be made, as well as the need to maintain vigilance against slipping backward under economic pressures on such matters as adverse trade balances and monetary crises.

The rest of this chapter is devoted to a brief account of where we have been, where we now stand, and what the future may hold on four major topics: international copyright, barriers to international trade, taxation of royalties, and postal and other transport charges.

INTERNATIONAL COPYRIGHT

After a hectic period of pressing problems and high level international negotiation in the years 1966-72, a time of relative calm has arrived—at least temporarily. The crisis during these last five years revolved around efforts of the so-called developing countries to secure sweeping relaxation of the copyright protection provided by the Berne and Universal Copyright Conventions under threat of withdrawal. Concessions to the developing countries were granted in the Protocol adopted by a revision conference for the Berne Convention in Stockholm in July, 1967. The Stockholm Protocol would have granted the developing countries in the Berne Convention the right to translate and reproduce copyright materials originating in a developed country for purposes of teaching, education, and research without the permission of the author or payment to the author and to export these translations and reproductions to other countries. Although the United States is not a member of the Berne Convention, had the Stockholm Protocol been ratified the same concessions would have incorporated into the Universal Convention under threat of the withdrawal of the developing countries. In addition, even before any modification of the U.C.C., United States copyright materials, now protected under the Berne Convention in some countries which are not members of the Universal Convention, would have been affected.

Following the lead of Great Britain, which made it quite clear that it would never ratify the Stockholm Protocol, other developed countries in

Berne took similar positions and it soon became obvious that the Protocol was dead. The United States took the initiative in an effort to draw up a set of lesser concessions to the developing countries, to be applied both in the Berne Convention and the Universal Convention. After many international meetings, a set of more limited concessions agreeable to all were developed and finally approved in a joint revision conference of the Berne and the Universal Conventions in Paris in July, 1971. We are now in the period of ratification of these revised Berne and Universal Conventions. This requires five ratifications to become operative as among the ratifying countries for Berne and twelve ratifications for the Universal Convention. In addition, ratification of the revised Universal Convention by the United Kingdom, Spain, France, and the United States is required before the revised Berne Convention can become operative. Thus far France, the United Kingdom, and the United States have ratified the revised Universal Convention; and France, the United Kingdom, and Hungary have ratified the revised Berne Convention.

Without going into detail, it can be said that the revised versions of Berne and the U.C.C. permit the developing countries to issue compulsory licenses for the translation, or the reproduction in the same language, of copyright materials originating in the developed countries if voluntary licenses cannot be agreed upon after a certain period of time has elapsed from the date of publication. These waiting periods are different for various categories of materials. The Universal Convention has always had a general provision permitting translations under compulsory licenses after seven years, but the provision has apparently never had to be used. Export of these compulsory licensed works is in general prohibited. Although some opposition to the ratification of the revised Universal Convention was expressed in hearings before the Senate Foreign Relations Committee in August, 1972, on the grounds that too many concessions were being granted to the developing countries, the Committee recommended the revised Convention unanimously and it was ratified by the Senate on August 14, 1972, by a vote of 67 to 0.

Thus the problem that threatened to torpedo the whole structure of international copyright has been met. What remains in the immediate future is implementation: ratification of the revised Berne and Universal Conventions, passage by the developing countries of domestic legislation defining procedures for compulsory licensing, and monitoring the new international structure when it comes into existence to see that it works out in practice in an equitable manner for all concerned. This transitional stage may well take several years.

In the longer run, it would seem desirable to marge the two international copyright conventions into one. One of the major obstacles to the accession of the United States to the Berne Convention has been the short period of copyright in the United States as compared with the requirement of the Berne Convention of the life of the author plus fifty years. If the United

States term of copyright—presently twenty-eight years from publication plus a renewal period of twenty-eight years—is extended to life plus fifty years as proposed in the general copyright revision bill under consideration in the Senate Judiciary Committee, prospects seem good that the adjustments could be made on certain other Berne requirements to permit the United States to join Berne. If this happens, other nonmembers of Berne in the Universal Convention will probably follow suit. It is possible that the general copyright revision bill will be acted upon by the Congress in 1974.

A word needs to be said also about recent action of the Soviet Union in adhering to the Universal Copyright Convention on May 27, 1973. This was a historic step since neither Imperial Russia nor the U.S.S.R. had assumed the obligation of respecting international copyright as a member of multilateral convention. There has been a good deal of public speculation as to whether, simultaneously, the U.S.S.R. was about to take steps to make it more difficult for dissident Soviet authors to publish their works outside the Soviet Union. Thus far this is speculation only, and even a liberal group within the U.S.S.R. has written to the Director General of the United Nations Educational, Scientific, and Cultural Organization (UNESCO) supporting Soviet accession to the U.C.C. and merely raising a warning signal about using the convention as a repressive measure. Vigilance is required, but there would seem to be great technical difficulties, as well as political problems, in any effort by the Soviet government to use the Universal Convention to impede publication of dissident Soviet authors in other countries.

FREE INTERNATIONAL FLOW OF MATERIALS

In 1967, after some fifteen years of consideration, the United States ratified the so-called Florence and Beirut Agreements (technically the Agreement on the Importation of Educational, Scientific, and Cultural Materials and the Agreement for Facilitating the International Circulation of Visual and Auditory Materials of Educational, Scientific, and Cultural Character). Some sixty-two countries are now members of Florence, which eliminates import duties and discriminatory taxation on a wide variety of educational and cultural materials, including books, magazines, newspapers, maps, music, original art, antiques, and under certain limitations audiovisual materials and scientific apparatus. The Beirut Agreement now has twenty-seven members. It contains the same provisions eliminating import duties and discriminatory taxation on audio and visual materials, such as educational films, certified by the countries of exportation as being of an educational, scientific, or cultural nature. In addition, the Beirut Agreement prohibits the imposition of quantitative restrictions, quotas, and import licenses on such certified audiovisual materials.

It was a historic step comparable to the U.S. ratification of the Universal Copyright Convention in 1955 when the United States acceded to the Flor-

34

ence and Beirut Agreements. The United States had imposed a tariff on books since 1791. This action marked recognition by the United States that publications and other educational and cultural materials were something more than mere commodities and, therefore, deserved a special free trade status.

Future policy questions in the area of the international flow of educational and cultural materials involve such matters as:

1. The extension of the Florence Agreement to the elimination of additional trade barriers such as import licenses, exchange restrictions, and new forms of taxation such as the import taxes equivalent to the Value Added Tax (VAT) now applied to books in all member countries except Britain of the European Economic Committee Community
2. The extension of duty-free treatment to the importation of equipment and materials essential to the local production of educational and cultural materials, such as printing machinery and paper for publications.

Because of the existence of the two agreements, questions of this type naturally lent themselves to consideration internationally as possible revisions and extensions of Florence and Beirut. The Director General of UNESCO, pursuant to the authorization of the General Conference of UNESCO in 1972, has called an international conference of experts in Geneva, Switzerland, for November, 1973, to consider the possible extension of the two agreements. Since this is a diplomatic conference consisting of government delegations, it will be up to the various governments participating to make proposals which could be recommended by the conference for later formal action by UNESCO.

International Taxation of Literary and Musical Royalties

Although no statistics are available, it is certain that there is much more access internationally to the works of writers and composers through local editions and translations of books, local recordings of music, and local performances of musical and dramatic works than through the export of actual books, recordings, and sheet music to other countries.

The existence of international copyright makes it possible for a publisher in another country to buy translation or reproduction rights; have protection for his investment in such rights so he can publish and sell his edition if necessary over a period of years; and provide the author or the original publisher some income. However, the original author or publisher may find that much of his royalty from the license of foreign rights is taxed away, not only in his own country but again in the country in which the translation or reproduction rights have been sold. The United States, for example, withholds 30 percent of the royalties of a foreign author selling translation or publication rights to American publishers unless the author is lucky enough to live in a country with which the United States has a general bilateral treaty or convention eliminating such double taxation.

Such treaties are commonly referred to as double taxation conventions, their purpose being to eliminate double taxation. The United States has these double taxation conventions with most of the developed countries of the world, but few conventions and little prospect of any more with the developing countries, which regard these general conventions covering a wide variety of economic transactions not to be in their financial interest. A similar network of bilateral double taxation conventions exists between other developed countries. It has been proposed that a multilateral double taxation convention limited to literary dramatic, musical, and other copyright royalties be created, either separately or as an addition or protocol to the Florence Agreement. It is felt that such a proposal might be regarded as advantageous and therefore acceptable to developed and developing countries alike. This suggestion may be taken up at the international conference of experts on the Florence and Beirut Agreements called by UNESCO for late 1973 in Geneva.

International Transportation Charges and Conditions—By Post and Sea and Air Freight

Transportation charges and speed of transportation are important factors in the international flow of books, magazines, and other published materials.

Because of the existence of the Universal Postal Union—dating from the nineteenth century—and the active intervention of UNESCO, progress has been made in the period since World War II in facilitating the international transmission of books, magazines, newspapers, and music through the mails. At the urging of UNESCO, the Universal Postal Union over two decades ago provided in the Universal Postal Convention (which is revised every five years) that national postal administrations might grant reductions in the international rates they charged for published materials, including music, up to 50 percent of their general rates for printed matter. (The Universal Postal Convention provides that national postal administrations must keep their international rates for the various specified classes of mail within a designated broad band or bracket.) The United States Post Office Department took advantage of this option, in response to the urgent recommendations of publishing organizations, library groups, and certain other federal agencies, in 1958, setting the international postal rates for books, magazines, and music at 50 percent of the general printed matter rate when sent to Canada and Mexico and at 66 percent of the general printed rate for the rest of the world.

There has also been a liberalization in the Universal Postal Convention, again at the urging of UNESCO, in the weight limits on book package in the international mails. This has been done by raising the limit on individual packages, and also by permitting the inclusion in mail sacks to one foreign address of numerous individually-wrapped packages.

To summarize, progress has been made in the postal field so far as

this would be costly and counterproductive. Given the amount of regionalization already in existence, our experience shows that it has been increasingly difficult to get up-to-date information and timely responses to our need for current data about ongoing library activities. Information dissemination has been almost nil since centralized reporting on library projects was eliminated here and parceled out to the 10 HEW regions.

In the budget message and other statements, the administration has confirmed the fact that libraries have used Federal support wisely and effectively. However, the administration position seems to be that in the future libraries should look to revenue sharing and to other broader assistance programs still on the drawing board instead of those with a demonstrated history of economy and efficiency. We contend that the possibility that new legislation may support libraries to some indeterminate extent at some unknown date in the future should not be swapped against the certainty that they can be continued on the sound basis of the past and present.

We are mindful of the fiscal stringency that faces the country and Congress at this time. Our member librariers are very much aware of the impact of inflation, the rising cost of many of the materials they must acquire, and the many other goods and services they must purchase. The cost of books alone has increased by 54 percent in the past 5 years, to an average of $12.99 for adults' books; children's books average $4.37. For this reason, we are not asking the subcommittee to approve large increases in our appropriations. On the other hand, we cannot accept their total elimination as proposed by the administration. That would cause sharp curtailment and in some cases a complete cutoff of library services throughout the Nation. Furthermore, in addition to proposing that the subcommittee maintain funding for library programs in fiscal year 1974 at the level in the vetoed Labor-HEW bill, H.R. 15417, we also strongly urge that the legislative history of the 1974 Appropriations Act make clear, in the report of this subcommittee and during floor debate, that the mandatory expenditure requirement of section 415 of the General Education Provisions Act is intended to apply to these and other education programs subject to section 415.

Currently operating under the ambiguous language of the continuing resolution (Public Law 92–334, as amended), HEW Secretary Weinberger has apparently decided to view the measure as a discretionary authority establishing a maximum or outer spending limit, not a fixed or mandatory one. Consequently, some library activities, deferred while awaiting final congressional action on a regular 1973 Labor-HEW Appropriations Act, are now having to be belatedly cut out. Equally appalling, hundreds of library employees connected with these federally funded programs are being laid off. According to preliminary data we are receiving from the State library agencies, some 2,300 people will be laid off in fiscal year 1974 if this situation prevails and if Congress does not reject the administration's proposals to zero out these essential library programs.

PUBLIC LIBRARIES

We recommend that $84.5 million be appropriated for programs authorized under the three titles of the Library Services and Construction Act (title I— Services, $62 million; title II—Construction, $15 million; title III—Interlibrary Cooperation, $7.5 million). In 1970 the President signed legislation extending these authorizations through 1976 and expressed his approval of the enactment when doing so. Under the 1970 amendments, each State is required to develop a comprehensive 5-year program for meeting the library and information needs of the people of the State. The basic State plans and the 5-year programs have recently been developed and all the States are proceeding to carry them out, meeting their needs as they determine them, in a systematic and orderly way, after consultation with their respective State advisory councils. We believe it is inconceivable that Congress and the administration would not keep faith with the States now with respect to the commitments they have made to the improvement of library services. Attached to this statement are tables showing the fiscal year 1973 LSCA allotments currently being received by the States according to the administration's budget as contrasted with what Congress intended under H.R. 15417. The committee must take prompt action to guard against the termination of these programs under a fiscal year 1974 continuing resolution based on this year's zero budget for libraries. Come July 1, another continuing resolution such

39

as we had this year would result in abrupt termination of all the library programs, and the staff with the necessary expertise to administer them moved elsewhere. Dollar amounts must be specified for each program.

To suggest, as the budget does, that general revenue sharing funds will provide support for the State library programs is to camouflage what amounts to an item veto in an appropriations bill. It is true that public libraries are listed among the eight "priority expenditures" programs of local government for which general revenue sharing funds may be used to cover operating expenses. However, the little information we have been able to get about the use of the early revenue sharing disbursements does not indicate that general revenue sharing is the answer to the pressing financial problems of libraries. In any event, spokesmen for the Treasury Department have stated that it will be 2 years before valid general conclusions may be drawn as to how general revenue sharing is working. For your information, we have attached to this statement charts to illustrate the preliminary library revenue sharing data we have thus far received and comments describing some of the reactions at the State and local levels. On first glance, the local allocations for construction looks quite promising, but many questions remain unanswered. For example, we find that in almost every State it is difficult to separate funds anticipated from those actually received. And in many instances recipient libraries have been warned not to expect additional money—they have had their turn.

Given the uncertainty of general revenue sharing at this time and the fact that its legislative history makes clear it was not intended to replace such categorical aid programs as LSCA, we ask that the committee recommend appropriation of $62 million under title I of the LSCA for matching grants to the States, the same funding level approved by Congress for the current fiscal year. These grants help the States improve public library services to communities or groups lacking access to a public library or receiving inadequate service. In Kentucky, for example, 7 small libraries were established in 1971 on a demonstration basis in 5 rural counties with a population of nearly 127,000. Bookmobile service was also provided, and the State used $51,500 of LSCA funds and added $95,900 of State funds. After 2 years of experience with public library service, the people of Estill, Mercer, and Greenup Counties petitioned for a library tax, and they will take over the support of these libraries and their further development.

Now, that is one example of the prudent and effective use of support under title I of LSCA. It is needed and working in the cities as well—in Philadelphia, Boston, and Chicago, for example—and it is supporting the "Right To Read" program initiated by the President. Wisconsin used 15 percent of its title I funds in 1 fiscal year to start its Right to Read program, for instance, and it is bringing library services to many disadvantaged groups of all kinds. The Iowa State Traveling Library and the Nebraska Library Commission, to cite another example, have joined forces to serve 3,000 urban Indians, two reservations, and an Indian hospital through a library program operated by a Sioux Indian. We submit that this is a sound and creative use of the support provided under title I, as well as proof of the wisdom of the decision of Congress and the President, through the 1970 amendments to give the States greater discretion in the use of these funds so priorities could be set locally and services provided to the people who need them most.

The law, as you know, provides that title I funds be used to extend public library services to the physically handicapped, among several other special groups in the population that required particular attention. If we mean to bring handicapped people into the mainstream of everyday life and help them to become self-reliant and self-supporting, if possible, then we cannot agree with the recommendation that title I funds be terminated, for we know there are millions of Americans eligible for specialized library services because of their physical handicaps and yet, at the end of the last fiscal year, there were less than 330,000 active borrowers of the Library of Congress talking books, braille books, tapes, and other special materials and reading aids. They can be helped, they are being helped under title I of LSCA.

For title II, which authorizes grants to the States for public library construction, we recommend appropriation of $15 million, which would maintain the level of support approved by Congress for the current year. This program, as you know, has been at a complete standstill because of the refusal of the administration to release any of the appropriated funds. There are an estimated 200 communities throughout the country with library construction projects in approval form, and with State and local matching funds available, and we cannot reconcile this manifest readiness of the people to improve their libraries with the unwillingness of the administration to release any of the matching funds appropriated by Congress for this purpose.

Under title III, which authorizes grants to the States for development of cooperative networks of libraries at local, regional, or inter-State levels, we propose appropriation of $7.5 million, the amount approved by Congress for the current year. This is a vital appropriation item. It helps eliminate duplication of effort and duplication of resources. It brings to the local library patron materials his nearest library does not have. It is a wholly appropriate use of Federal funds, for it enables libraries to cooperate across State boundaries in many places—such as the metropolitan areas that straddle a State line—and in many ways. We consider its discontinuance, as proposed in the budget, to be completely incompatible with the emphasis in the budget on modernization and improvements in efficiency and economy in the provision of human services. Revenue sharing is totally unsuitable as a substitute for title III. The title III incentive for cooperation across governmental jurisdiction has no counterpart in revenue sharing which directs money to individual cities and towns. In fact, it may have just the opposite effect by forcing localities to be concerned solely with local projects.

SCHOOL LIBRARIES

Turning now to title II of the Elementary and Secondary Education Act, which authorizes grants to the States for school library resources, textbooks, and other instructional materials, we recommend appropriation of $100 million, which would maintain this program at the level approved by Congress for the current fiscal year. This program is another candidate for extinction selected by the administration, despite its outstanding accomplishments in the last 8 years and without regard to the immense needs that are still to be met.

The States report that on the average nearly one-third of their elementary schools lack libraries, and the Office of Education reported in 1970 that no more than half the secondary schools in any State met the standards for school libraries set by the States themselves. Attached is a map showing progress made since 1965 as well as the needs that remain. Also attached are comments highlighting these needs.

The budget tells us that title II is no longer needed because education revenue sharing will provide the necessary funding. As you know, though, education revenue sharing has not yet been enacted. It may be enacted, and in its final form it may contain some assurance that school libraries and textbooks and other instructional materials will get to the schools that need them. All this is many months in the future, if at all. In the meantime, children are in the classrooms, and school boards are drawing up their budgets for the school year that starts this fall. It would be tragic as well as myopic to halt an effective and sound program because new legislation has been proposed.

The highest courts of six States have concurred in the opinion of the California court that the school financing system must be changed to assure greater equality of educational opportunity instead of the great disparity of support for the schools that is found from district to district in many States. The U.S. Supreme Court has declared that, for the foreseeable future at least, it will be up to the States to achieve a higher degree of equalization in school expenditures. Suits are pending in many States that could result in additional judicial mandates for reform on school finance systems. Title II is a useful tool in the hands of a State legislature and Governor who seek equal educational opportunities. Indeed, the language of title II requires that the grants to the States be used within the State on the basis of the relative need of children and teachers for school library resources, textbooks, and other instructional materials. So this is inherently an equalizing program, among States and within States.

Two other favorable features of title II should be noted. First, these grants must be used to secure additional books and materials for learning. These funds cannot be used to replace other expenditures. Second, children in the nonpublic schools benefit from the program. Dr. Sidney P. Marland, the Assistant Secretary for Education, stated in January 1973: "Virtually all nonpublic authorities, I understand, are happy with their treatment under title II of ESEA which provides books and other learning materials * * *. The program has come to be regarded by the nonpublic sector as providing the highest

41

degree of equity for their children. Our figures for fiscal year 1973 show
5,300,000 nonpublic children participating—or 98 percent of those eligible.
And the average annual title II expenditure per participating pupil is, by our
latest accounting, exactly the same for both—$1.92." Again, we cannot square
the proposal of the budget that title II programs be terminated with the
policy enunciated several times by the President that the maximum assistance
consistent with the Constitution be extended to the nonpublic schools.

We would point out also that title II funds are undergirding the "Right To
Read" program, which the Budget quite properly gives the status of a "national
priority" program. Almost 30 percent of all title II funds obtained by the schools
in the last fiscal year were targeted for "Right To Read" projects. Moreover,
the Title II programs are effective, by objective measurement. A $3,000 pro-
gram in the Baldwin City, Kansas, High School is one good example among
many others. When the students were polled, 80 percent said they want more
materials to study and special instruction to improve their reading. After the
library materials and special instruction were provided through the $3,000
grant, almost every one raised his or her reading scores. The correlation between accessibility of reading material and special instruction on the one
hand, and improved reading ability on the other, was unmistakable among
this group of students all of whom had previously read one or more years below
their grade level.

Not only are the title II funds demonstrably effective, but their use is also
soundly coordinated with other assistance provided by this committee, particularly the funds available under title III–A of the National Defense Education
Act for classroom equipment. ESEA title II often provides the software to be
used with instructional equipment acquired under NDEA title III. NDEA title
III subject specialists are frequently asked for consultative help in selection,
organization, and use of materials to be bought with ESEA II funds. Hundreds
of projects making intelligent use of modern equipment, materials, and tech-
niques have improved the learning conditions of countless students. Accordingly,
we recommend that the appropriation for the matching grants under title III–A
of NDEA also be maintained at the level voted by Congress for the current fiscal
year, that is, $50 million. We do not agree that this program should be termi-
nated.

HIGHER EDUCATION

By the same token, we cannot concede that support for college and university
libraries and for library training and research, which is authorized by title II,
parts A and B, of the Higher Education Act, should be terminated as proposed
in the budget. When the budget was made public, the HEW Department at-
tempted to justify elimination of these programs in this manner : "Recent amendments to the legislative authorities for these programs have made it impossible
to set funding priorities and, in the case of college libraries, to provide meaningful levels of assistance."

Here, the Congress has repeatedly and explicitly told the Office of Education
how parts A and B of title II should be administered, and yet year after year
the Office asserts it cannot or will not carry out the very clear legislative intent.
Although they were given a very short period in which to apply for the title II–A
college library resources grants, over 2,300 colleges and universities have filed
applications for the fiscal year 1973 basic grants to which they are entitled according to Public Law 92–318 (the Education Amendments of 1972). These basic
grants of up to $5,000 per institution must be matched dollar for dollar by the
applicant institutions. This is ample evidence, we submit, that these grants are
needed and will be put to good use. Attached for your information is a map showing for each State the estimated basic grant entitlements.

We recommend appropriation of $30 million in fiscal year 1974 for title II—
with 70 percent for part A and 30 percent for part B, as specified in Public Law
92–318. This will provide $21 million for college library resources under part A.
In our estimation, this will permit the Commissioner of Education to provide
some supplemental grants to the neediest institutions as well as special purpose
matching grants to encourage greater sharing of library materials among
institutions.

The grants available under title II–A have permitted many smaller colleges to
improve the support given by their libraries to graduate programs without limit-
ing support of the undergraduate programs. A notable development under title
II–A has been the formation of consortia of the libraries of a group of colleges
and universities in the same general area. One directory has identified 125 formal,

42

cooperative arrangements of this kind among the libraries of higher education.
There are 23 member institutions in the Northwest Association of Private Colleges and Universities, to describe one of these consortia. They are located in
Oregon, Washington, Montana, Idaho and Utah, and one member college is in
Alaska. The Association's headquarters is in Portland, Oreg. The association has
received several annual grants under title II–A for the mutual benefit of the
member institutions and their students and teachers. When items are needed by
the cooperating libraries, they are borrowed from the central facility donated by
Lewis and Clark College in Portland. They have thus been able to fill gaps in
their individual collections, to offer superior service to their users, and in some
cases to help some of their academic departments qualify for accreditation.

We believe this is the way this committee and the taxpayers want to see Federal assistance utilized, and we can assure you that this is the way the funds
you make available under title II–A have been used and should be used in the
future.

Under title II-part B, the 30 percent remaining of the $30 million we recom-
mend would provide $6 million for training in librarianship and $3 million for
research and demonstration grants to improve libraries and information science.
For 1974, the budget proposes termination of these programs, and the reason
given by the HEW Department when the budget was made public is that the
authorizing legislation "mandates the use of appropriated funds for both fellowships and institute training programs in such a way that Federal appropriations
cannot be easily adapted to changing manpower requirements."

For our part, we cannot fathom this explanation. The law requires that at least
half the training funds be used for fellowships and traineeships. The other half
may be used for other and shorter courses of training or study. It seems to us
that the statute affords ample administrative discretion. Certainly, training in
librarianship and information science is needed at the paraprofessional, master's
and postmaster's levels, and many practicing librarians need to update their
skills and knowledge. The computer and cable television are only two of the new
technologies that are changing many libraries. Managing the interlibrary networks and consortia calls for advanced training. The Nation's library schools are
not producing enough Ph. D. librarians to meet the requirements of their own
faculties due to normal attrition, much less producing enough of the very highly
qualified librarians we need to administer the major institutions and perform
research of the highest quality. (See attached comments on library training.)

The nature of the library research and demonstration program is not always
fully understood, though it is simpler essentially than many of the other research programs reviewed and supported by this committee. To present one example, Congress has directed that library services be extended to the elderly, the
mentally ill, and other persons living in institutions. What is the most effective
way to provide library services in these institutions? The Rhode Island Department of State Library Services is using a title II–B grant to study alternate tech-
niques of providing library services to the elderly patients at the Institute of
Mental Health. Should the approach be to individuals or to groups of patients?
Should patients be allowed to ignore the availability of the library, or should
they be encouraged to visit the library? How can use of the library help improve
the outlook and behavior of the patients? What should the library personnel staff
do, and what should the other staff members of the institution and its volunteers
do, to make the library program as effective as possible? These are the kinds of
questions this research effort is trying to answer, and its findings will be useful,
of course, in all other States.

Another library research project, this one at the North Texas State University
at Denton, is studying the feasibility of merging the public library and the school
library services in the rural community of Olney, Tex. The financial and legal
aspects have to be explored in advance, as well as the library's facilities and
functions, to determine whether a combined school and public library would be
more effective than the customary pattern. Again, the findings of this research
project will be of value to school boards and boards of library trustees throughout the country.

HIGHER EDUCATION ACT, TITLE III

We support the administration's recommendation of $99 million for fiscal year
1974 for this program of special assistance to strengthen the academic quality of
developing institutions. HEA III funds may be used, among other purposes, for

43

joint use of academic facilities such as libraries, including necessary books, materials, and equipment. Title III funds can thus provide a much-needed supplement to strengthen the library resources and service of developing institutions so often neglected in the past.

HIGHER EDUCATION ACT, TITLE VI

Another program in which college and university libraries may participate is title VI of the Higher Education Act which authorizes a program to improve the quality of undergraduate instruction by providing financial assistance on a matching basis to institutions of higher education for the acquisition of instructional equipment, materials, and related minor remodelnig. Accordingly, we recommend an appropriation of $12.5 million for this program in fiscal year 1974, the same amount appropriated by Congress last year.

NATIONAL CENTER FOR EDUCATIONAL STATISTICS

The association supports the work of the National Center for Educational Statistics as it relates to libraries, and urges that NCES receive an adequate fiscal year 1974 appropriation so that it is able to continue and improve its program of gathering, storing, analyzing, and disseminating educational information, including data on all types of libraries. Basic, comparable statistical information about all types of library service is absolutely essential to a rational determination of the needs and most effective use of all our Nation's libraries.

EDUCATIONAL RESOURCES INFORMATION CENTER

We support the work of the National Institute of Education's Educational Resources Information Center, particularly its clearinghouse on library and information sciences, which has responsibiltiy for acquiring, organizing, and making available research-related documents and journal articles in the field of library and information sciences. We request that an adequate appropriation be made for the program in fiscal year 1974 so that this vital information service can be continued and improved.

OTHER PROGRAMS

To continue, the American Library Association also urges the committee to accept the recommendation of the budget that $25 million be appropriated for the National Library of Medicine and the Medical Library Assistance Act. We also support the goals of the National Commission on Libraries and Information Science and recommend that the full authorization of $750,000 be appropriated for fiscal year 1974. The Commission has been hampered in its beginning phases by limited means with which to carry out the extensive program set for it by Congress, and we are appreciative of the past support of the Commission's plans given by the administration.

In conclusion, we would emphasize two factors that apply to all the library programs supported by the appropriations in this bill. First, they are not programs in which the Federal authorities dictate to States or communities or private institutions and organizations. An application must be filed for every one of these grants; there is nothing automatic about receipt of these funds. That means that a number of people at local and State levels must agree on the need for these library programs, and the priorities for funding are set in the first instance in the State, not in Washington. What's more, most of these programs require matching funds, which represents a commitment of a different sort. So we believe the library programs funded in this bill are the kind the administration should favor, in keeping with its aim to return power to the people, programs under private as well as public auspices, in which local people decide how they want to use their tax money.

Second, we want to emphasize that the library programs supported in this bill undergrid and strengthen nearly all the other programs funded through the Labor-HEW Appropriations Act. Libraries serve disadvantaged children and adults, libraries help all the millions of college students who will be aided through this bill, libraries are essential in the health professions training programs, and the biomedical and other research programs. Thus the library programs in this bill do not stand alone. If they are weakened, as the budget pro-

44

posals would do, nearly all the other programs of the bill would also be weakened to some extent, some of them gravely. On the other hand, investment in the library programs enhances the effectiveness of funds you appropriate for other purposes.

While our testimony has been devoted primarily to the needs of library programs, we would like the record to show as well that we endorse the statement to be presented to you on behalf of the Committee for Full Funding of Education Programs.

Thank you, Mr. Chairman and members of the committee, for this opportunity to present testimony on behalf of the American Library Association. We urge your favorable consideration of our request for a realistic level of funding for vital library and education programs.

FUNDS FOR LIBRARY-RELATED PROGRAMS

	FY '72 Appropriation	FY '73 Appropriation[1]	FY '73 Allocation[2]	FY '74 Authorization	FY '74 Budget Recommendation
Elementary and Secondary Education Act					
Title I - Educationally Deprived Children	$1,597,500,000	$1,810,000,000	$1,585,185,000	(Based on formula)[3]	-0- *[/]
II - School Library Resources, Textbooks, and Other Instructional Materials	90,000,000	100,000,000	90,000,000	220,000,000[3]	-0- T[/]
III - Suppl. Educ. Centers, Guidance, Counseling and Testing	146,393,000	171,393,000	146,393,000	605,000,000[3]	-0- *[/]
V-A Strengthening State Educ. Depts.	33,000,000	53,000,000	33,000,000	90,000,000[3]	-0- T[/]
VI-B Education of Handicapped Children	37,500,000	65,000,000	37,500,000	220,000,000[3]	-0- *[/]
VII Bilingual Education Programs	35,000,000	60,000,000	35,080,000	135,000,000[3]	$35,800,000
Library Services and Construction Act	58,709,000	84,500,000	32,730,000	228,000,000	-0- T[/]
Title I - Library Services	46,568,500	62,000,000	30,000,000	123,500,000	-0-
II - Public Library Construction	9,500,000	15,000,000	-0-	88,000,000	-0-
III - Interlibrary Cooperation	2,640,500	7,500,000	2,730,000	16,500,000	-0-
National Defense Education Act					
Title III-A Instructional Assistance	50,000,000	50,000,000	1,500,000	130,500,000	-0- T[/]
VI - Language Development	15,300,000	-0- [4]	-0- [4]	75,000,000	1,360,000
Higher Education Act					
Title I - Community Service Program	9,500,000	15,000,000[5]	5,700,000[6]	40,000,000	-0- T[/]
II - Parts A & B	15,750,000	17,857,000[5]	15,000,000[6]	85,000,000	-0- T[/]
Part A - College Library Resources)	11,000,000	12,500,000	10,500,000	59,500,000	-0-
B - Library Training)	2,000,000	3,572,000	3,000,000	17,000,000	-0-
Research)	2,750,000	1,785,000	1,500,000	8,500,000	-0-
C - LC Acquisition & Cataloging	7,145,000	7,667,138[7]	7,667,138[7]	15,000,000	8,500,000
III - Developing Institutions	51,850,000	-0- [4]	-0- [4]	120,000,000	99,992,000
V - Education Professions Development	135,800,000	121,600,000	118,600,000[8]	300,000,000	73,475,000
VI-A Equipment & Matls. for Higher Ed.	12,500,000	12,500,000	-0-	60,000,000	-0- T[/]
National Library of Medicine and Medical Library Assistance Act)	24,127,000	28,818,000	25,074,000[9]	(42 USC 275 and need new auth.)	24,994,000
National Commission on Libraries and Inf. Sc.	200,000	406,000	406,000	750,000	406,000
Right to Read Program	-0-	12,000,000	12,000,000	-0-	12,000,000

---

[1]/ Unless otherwise noted, based on Congressional intent in HR 15417 passed and sent to White House 8/10/72 and Continuing Resolution (PL 92-334 as amended).
[2]/ Unless otherwise noted based on the Administration's interpretation of Continuing Resolution (PL 92-334 as amended).
[3]/ Based on one-year automatic extension in General Education Provisions Act, Sec. 413(c).
[4]/ Pending Congressional action on FY 1973 supplemental request submitted 1/29/73.
[5]/ Supplemental appropriations (PL 92-607).
[6]/ President's requested rescission submitted to Congress 1/29/73.
[7]/ Legislative appropriations (PL 92-342).
[8]/ Of total, $81,165,000 in supplemental (PL 92-607) and $37,435,000 under Continuing Resolution (PL 92-334 as amended).
[9]/ Based on President's budget request as revised 1/29/73.

*To be absorbed by proposed education revenue sharing.   T - To be terminated.

May 1973

<u>Estimated Grants for Library Services--LSCA Title I</u>
(Note: totals include outlying territories not listed)

	1972 Appropriation	1973 Allocation[1]	1973 Appropriation[2]	1974 Budget
TOTALS	$46,568,500	$30,000,000	$62,000,000	Zero
Alabama	801,520	524,744	1,059,361	-0-
Alaska	252,774	228,491	275,396	-0-
Arizona	509,562	367,124	642,256	-0-
Arkansas	535,902	381,344	679,885	-0-
California	3,684,797	2,081,346	5,170,548	-0-
Colorado	585,496	408,119	750,738	-0-
Connecticut	729,574	485,902	956,575	-0-
Delaware	295,726	251,680	336,759	-0-
Dist. of Col.	332,124	271,330	388,758	-0-
Florida	1,385,770	840,165	1,894,048	-0-
Georgia	1,001,565	632,743	1,345,154	-0-
Hawaii	334,465	272,594	392,103	-0-
Idaho	324,526	267,228	377,904	-0-
Illinois	2,141,046	1,247,917	2,973,071	-0-
Indiana	1,107,070	689,702	1,495,883	-0-
Iowa	693,391	466,368	904,882	-0-
Kansas	592,798	412,061	761,170	-0-
Kentucky	762,250	503,543	1,003,257	-0-
Louisiana	836,278	543,509	1,109,017	-0-
Maine	373,542	293,691	447,931	-0-
Maryland	885,043	569,836	1,178,686	-0-
Massachusetts	1,193,608	736,422	1,619,517	-0-
Michigan	1,750,025	1,036,816	2,414,440	-0-
Minnesota	864,552	558,773	1,149,411	-0-
Mississippi	587,182	409,029	753,146	-0-
Missouri	1,016,903	641,024	1,367,068	-0-
Montana	321,278	265,475	373,263	-0-
Nebraska	459,143	339,904	570,224	-0-
Nevada	285,358	246,082	321,946	-0-
New Hampshire	328,835	269,555	384,060	-0-
New Jersey	1,451,913	875,874	1,988,543	-0-
New Mexico	377,443	295,797	453,504	-0-
New York	3,376,997	1,915,172	4,738,809	-0-
North Carolina	1,087,577	679,178	1,468,035	-0-
North Dakota	307,891	258,248	354,139	-0-
Ohio	2,060,365	1,204,360	2,857,807	-0-
Oklahoma	646,971	441,307	838,565	-0-
Oregon	565,258	397,193	721,826	-0-
Pennsylvania	2,259,795	1,312,027	3,142,723	-0-
Rhode Island	365,868	289,548	436,967	-0-
South Carolina	652,431	444,255	846,365	-0-
South Dakota	316,361	262,820	366,239	-0-
Tennessee	885,352	570,003	1,179,126	-0-
Texas	2,155,499	1,255,720	2,993,719	-0-
Utah	385,001	299,877	464,301	-0-
Vermont	277,672	241,933	310,966	-0-
Virginia	1,011,855	638,298	1,359,855	-0-
Washington	795,408	521,445	1,050,629	-0-
West Virginia	504,629	364,461	635,208	-0-
Wisconsin	971,588	616,559	1,302,328	-0-
Wyoming	258,056	231,343	282,942	-0-

American Library Association
Washington Office
May, 1973

[1]/ Based on President's FY 1973 Budget.
[2]/ Based on Congressional intent in HR 15417
passed and sent to White House August 10, 1972,
and Continuing Resolution (PL 92-334, as amended).

Estimated Grants for Library Construction--LSCA Title II
(Note: totals include outlying territories not listed)

	1972 Appropriation	1973 Allocation[1]	1973 Appropriation[2]	1974 Budget
TOTALS	$9,500,000	-0-	$15,000,000	Zero
Alabama	170,495	-0-	262,383	-0-
Alaska	106,185	-0-	114,247	-0-
Arizona	136,279	-0-	183,568	-0-
Arkansas	139,366	-0-	190,678	-0-
California	508,399	-0-	1,040,735	-0-
Colorado	145,178	-0-	204,066	-0-
Connecticut	162,063	-0-	242,961	-0-
Delaware	111,219	-0-	125,842	-0-
Dist. of Col.	115,484	-0-	135,667	-0-
Florida	238,966	-0-	420,104	-0-
Georgia	193,939	-0-	316,386	-0-
Hawaii	115,759	-0-	136,299	-0-
Idaho	114,594	-0-	133,616	-0-
Illinois	327,480	-0-	623,994	-0-
Indiana	206,304	-0-	344,867	-0-
Iowa	157,823	-0-	233,193	-0-
Kansas	146,034	-0-	206,038	-0-
Kentucky	165,893	-0-	251,782	-0-
Louisiana	174,568	-0-	271,766	-0-
Maine	120,338	-0-	146,849	-0-
Maryland	180,283	-0-	284,931	-0-
Massachusetts	216,445	-0-	368,229	-0-
Michigan	281,654	-0-	518,436	-0-
Minnesota	177,882	-0-	279,399	-0-
Mississippi	145,376	-0-	204,521	-0-
Missouri	195,737	-0-	320,527	-0-
Montana	114,213	-0-	132,740	-0-
Nebraska	130,370	-0-	169,957	-0-
Nevada	110,003	-0-	123,043	-0-
New Hampshire	115,099	-0-	134,780	-0-
New Jersey	246,717	-0-	437,960	-0-
New Mexico	120,795	-0-	147,902	-0-
New York	472,327	-0-	957,643	-0-
North Carolina	204,019	-0-	339,605	-0-
North Dakota	112,644	-0-	129,126	-0-
Ohio	318,025	-0-	602,214	-0-
Oklahoma	152,383	-0-	220,662	-0-
Oregon	142,806	-0-	198,603	-0-
Pennsylvania	341,396	-0-	656,051	-0-
Rhode Island	119,439	-0-	144,777	-0-
South Carolina	153,022	-0-	222,136	-0-
South Dakota	113,637	-0-	131,412	-0-
Tennessee	180,319	-0-	285,014	-0-
Texas	329,174	-0-	627,896	-0-
Utah	121,681	-0-	149,942	-0-
Vermont	109,103	-0-	120,968	-0-
Virginia	195,145	-0-	319,164	-0-
Washington	169,779	-0-	260,733	-0-
West Virginia	135,701	-0-	182,236	-0-
Wisconsin	190,426	-0-	308,294	-0-
Wyoming	106,804	-0-	115,673	-0-

American Library Association
Washington Office
May, 1973

1/ Based on President's FY 1973 Budget.
2/ Based on Congressional intent in HR 15417
passed and sent to White House August 10, 1972,
and Continuing Resolution (PL 92-334, as amended).

Estimated Grants for Interlibrary Cooperation--LSCA Title III
(Note: totals include outlying territories not listed)

	1972 Appropriation	1973 Allocation[1]	1973 Appropriation[2]	1974 Budget
TOTALS	$2,640,500	$2,730,000	$7,500,000	Zero
Alabama	48,695	50,190	129,879	-0-
Alaska	40,763	40,894	47,885	-0-
Arizona	44,475	45,244	86,255	-0-
Arkansas	44,855	45,690	90,190	-0-
California	90,372	99,034	560,695	-0-
Colorado	45,572	46,530	97,600	-0-
Connecticut	47,655	48,971	119,129	-0-
Delaware	41,384	41,622	54,303	-0-
Dist. of Col.	41,910	42,238	59,742	-0-
Florida	57,140	60,087	217,177	-0-
Georgia	51,587	53,579	159,769	-0-
Hawaii	41,944	42,278	60,092	-0-
Idaho	41,800	42,110	58,607	-0-
Illinois	68,058	72,882	330,030	-0-
Indiana	53,112	55,366	175,534	-0-
Iowa	47,132	48,358	113,722	-0-
Kansas	45,678	46,654	98,692	-0-
Kentucky	48,127	49,525	124,011	-0-
Louisiana	49,197	50,779	135,072	-0-
Maine	42,509	42,940	65,931	-0-
Maryland	49,902	51,605	142,359	-0-
Massachusetts	54,363	56,832	188,464	-0-
Michigan	62,405	66,258	271,604	-0-
Minnesota	49,606	51,258	139,297	-0-
Mississippi	45,597	46,559	97,852	-0-
Missouri	51,808	53,839	162,061	-0-
Montana	41,753	42,055	58,121	-0-
Nebraska	43,746	44,390	78,721	-0-
Nevada	41,234	41,446	52,754	-0-
New Hampshire	41,862	42,183	59,250	-0-
New Jersey	58,096	61,208	227,060	-0-
New Mexico	42,565	43,006	66,513	-0-
New York	85,923	93,820	514,704	-0-
North Carolina	52,830	55,036	172,621	-0-
North Dakota	41,560	41,828	56,121	-0-
Ohio	66,891	71,515	317,974	-0-
Oklahoma	46,461	47,572	106,786	-0-
Oregon	45,280	46,188	94,577	-0-
Pennsylvania	69,774	74,894	347,773	-0-
Rhode Island	42,398	42,810	64,784	-0-
South Carolina	46,540	47,664	107,602	-0-
South Dakota	41,682	41,971	57,387	-0-
Tennessee	49,907	51,610	142,405	-0-
Texas	68,266	73,127	332,189	-0-
Utah	42,674	43,134	67,643	-0-
Vermont	41,123	41,316	51,606	-0-
Virginia	51,735	53,753	161,307	-0-
Washington	48,607	50,086	128,965	-0-
West Virginia	44,403	45,161	85,517	-0-
Wisconsin	51,153	53,071	155,290	-0-
Wyoming	40,839	40,983	48,675	-0-

American Library Association
Washington Office
May, 1973

1/ Based on President's FY 1973 Budget.
2/ Based on Congressional intent in HR 15417 passed and sent to White House August 10, 1972, and Continuing Resolution (PL 92-334, as amended).

49

<u>Need for Adequate Appropriations for LSCA in FY 1974</u>
Based on reports from Libraries Across the Nation in 1973

PENNSYLVANIA Assuming zero funding of LSCA, the following services to specialized
groups would be terminated: Statewide film service from two regional
film libraries, Action Library in Philadelphia, Media Library for pre-schoolers in
Erie, and mail order delivery service for rural counties. Groups suffering most would
be aged, homebound, institutionalized, foreign born, ethnic minorities, inner city
poor, all of whom are aided by special projects at one or more location. Sixteen
State Library employees plus 24 persons now employed by libraries carrying out LSCA
projects would lose their jobs.

NEW JERSEY Lack of LSCA funding would eliminate this State's efforts to retrain, em-
ploy and recruit minority and disadvantaged persons; would remove major
capabilities to develop and provide effective development of model collections and to
extend supportive library services to day care centers, State, county and municipal
institutions, migrant workers, senior citizens and large centers of urban and rural
poor.

WISCONSIN Only about 50 percent of the State's population is covered by the public
library systems eligible for State aid. We do not have State funds to
continue statewide programs. Nor can the state funds easily be directed at high priority special needs such as interlibrary cooperation, interstate cooperation, continuing education, disadvantaged and handicapped. The American Indian communities, such as
Menominee County, will be badly hurt if LSCA is not funded.

OREGON Without LSCA the State Library would have to cut back drastically on programs
for supplementing the local public library resources and in providing direct
services to those without access to a local public library. Thirty-one positions
would be cut from the State library staff. The groups that would suffer most include
the blind and physically handicapped, persons in State institutions and Oregonians who
have no local public library services.

VIRGINIA Public libraries serving 4 million persons receive federal grants-in-aid
under LSCA. The major portion of this is used for materials which are
essential for the services offered by the libraries to all patrons. Without federal
funding most public library programs designed for special groups such as the aged, de-
linquents, and pre-school children will have to be dropped because the libraries will
not be able to support both staffing and materials.

TEXAS LSCA has been the incentive for better libraries all over the state. In Texas,
library support from the local communities increased from 54¢ per capita to
$2.08 in 1972. Even with this progress, libraries are not ready to be self-sufficient.
This is a time when libraries are reaching out and responding to changing needs of
society. We need the guidelines as well as the dollars from the federal government.

ILLINOIS By using our federal LSCA funds in 1965-1969 almost exclusively for developing our public library regional network, we were able to organize and provide services. We did, however, phase out all of our federal funds and replace them
with state funds for basic support of the library systems. Our LSCA funds, however,
are still essential because these are the only funds we have that can be used to
encourage cooperation between types of libraries and for the development of special
programs and services to disadvantaged, the aged, and institutionalized. Federal
funds as a means of stimulating and starting new ideas are essential.

KENTUCKY In FY 1973, low-level funding of LSCA under the continuing resolution meant
that new films were not purchased, needed new books were cut from orders,
worn-out equipment was not replaced, staff members who resigned often were not replaced.
If all federal funds are withdrawn the whole program will have to be cut back even
further. There are still 15 counties which have no public library or bookmobile services, and over 60 new library buildings are needed.

*   *   *

American Library Association
Washington Office
May, 1973

50

<u>**GENERAL REVENUE SHARING: A REPLACEMENT FOR LSCA?**</u>

N.B.   Although the legislative history of general revenue sharing makes clear
that it is not intended as a replacement for categorical aid such as LSCA,
the 1974 Budget ignores this fact in recommending zero funding of LSCA.

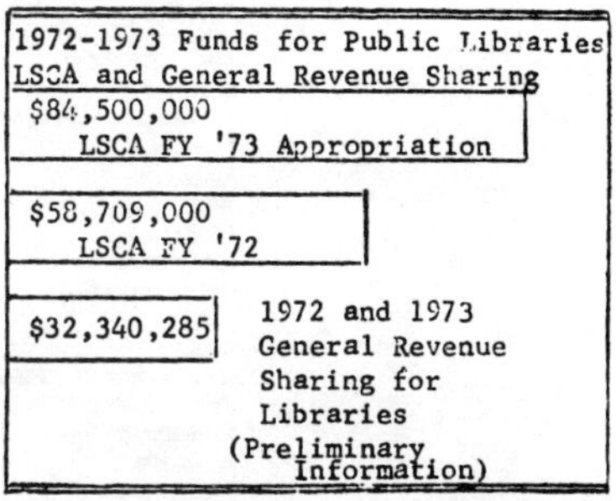

<u>The Library Services and Construction Act (LSCA)</u>
Authorized through June 30, 1976

<u>The State and Local Fiscal Assistance Act</u>
(General Revenue Sharing)
Authorized through December 31, 1976

<u>A Comparison</u>

<u>Purpose</u>.   Each Act is designed to accomplish an
entirely different purpose.

<u>LSCA</u> - "An Act to promote the further development
of public library services"

<u>General Revenue Sharing</u> - "An Act to provide fiscal
assistance to State and local governments"

1972-1973 Funds for Public Libraries LSCA and General Revenue Sharing
$84,500,000   LSCA FY '73 Appropriation
$58,709,000   LSCA FY '72
$32,340,285 — 1972 and 1973 General Revenue Sharing for Libraries (Preliminary Information)

<u>Basis for Comparison</u>.   LSCA and general revenue sharing are inherently not comparable
because one is a program of grants to the States for library development purposes, while
the other provides funds to all units of government, local and State, for general fiscal
assistance.

Because libraries may benefit from both, however, and because the 1974 Budget recommends
zero-funding of LSCA as an unnecessary program now that general revenue sharing is enacted, the two are compared on the attached charts which show dollars received by each
State under LSCA and within each State under general revenue sharing.   The purposes for
which the funds are spent are also shown.

<u>Chart No. 1</u> compares FY 1972 funds for library resources and services and for inter-
library cooperation under LSCA titles I and III, with funds for the same purposes allocated from 1972 and 1973 general revenue sharing entitlements.

<u>Chart No. 2</u> compares FY 1972 funds for library construction under LSCA title II with
funds for the same purpose allocated from 1972 and 1973 general revenue sharing entitlements.

To date, two-thirds of the <u>general revenue sharing</u> devoted to library purposes has been
for capital expenditures.   Ninety-four percent has come from units of local government,
the rest from State governments.   Whether these trends will be borne out in the years
to come, and at what rate, or indeed whether libraries will continue to receive
revenue sharing funds, are unknown factors.   Preliminary information indicates that in
many parts of the country revenue sharing for libraries is being used to offset county
or municipal budget cuts, supplanting rather than supplementing local library support.

<u>LSCA</u>, since the 1970 amendments, has been directed toward improved statewide and inter-
state cooperation to meet the library and information needs of all the American people.
In FY 1972, 96 percent of LSCA funds were in the form of matching grants.   In order to
participate in any LSCA program, each State must develop a comprehensive 5-year plan on
State priorities, procedures and activities for meeting the library needs of the people.
Each State must create a broadly representative State Advisory Council to assist in
developing the plan.   Improved coordination and cooperation among all types of libraries
crossing jurisdictional boundaries to eliminate costly duplication of resources and effort are primary goals of LSCA.

*   *   *

American Library Association
Washington Office
May, 1973

51

Chart 1 — Comparison of **LSCA** (FY 1972) and General Revenue Sharing (Estimated 1972-73) for Public Library Services and Resources, and for Interlibrary Cooperation.

(Dollars in Thousands)

STATES	LSCA[1]	Revenue Sharing[2]
Alabama	850,215	867,266
Alaska	293,537	· 0 ·
Arizona	554,037	56,418
Arkansas	580,757	109,467
California	3,775,169	132,585
Colorado	631,068	121,054
Connecticut	777,229	5,000
Delaware	337,110	· 0 ·
District of Columbia	374,034	· 0 ·
Florida	1,442,910	425,000
Georgia	1,053,152	223,134
Hawaii	376,409	· 0 ·
Idaho	366,326	3,000
Illinois	2,209,104	1,262,614
Indiana	1,160,182	· 0 ·
Iowa	740,523	65,000
Kansas	638,476	27,165
Kentucky	810,377	275,699
Louisiana	885,475	352,942
Maine	416,051	19,300
Maryland	934,945	24,000
Massachusetts	1,247,971	437,000
Michigan	1,812,430	1,095,369
Minnesota	914,158	193,585
Mississippi	632,779	24,900
Missouri	1,068,711	75,000
Montana	363,031	2,000
Nebraska	502,889	175
Nevada	326,592	38,000
New Hampshire	370,697	34,750
New Jersey	1,510,009	1,020,000
New Mexico	420,008	27,855
New York	3,462,920	65,950
North Carolir	1,140,407	345,570
North Dako	349,451	3,700
Ohio	2,127,256	116,324
Oklahoma	693,432	56,400
Oregon	610,538	805,000
Pennsylvania	2,329,569	212,000
Rhode Island	408,266	42,060
South Carolina	698,971	211,112
South Dakota	358,043	11,929
Tennessee	935,259	Unknown
Texas	2,223,765	132,000
Utah	427,675	· 0 ·
Vermont	318,795	15,000
Virginia	1,063,590	67,028
Washington	844,015	1,059,446
West Virginia	549,032	147,438
Wisconsin	1,022,741	365,800
Wyoming	298,895	· 0 ·
American Samoa	54,920	· 0 ·
Guam	65,401	· 0 ·
Puerto Rico	720,501	· 0 ·
Trust Territory	67,999	· 0 ·
Virgin Islands	61,198	· 0 ·
TOTALS	$49,209,000[1]	$10,575,035[2]

[1] LSCA grants awarded in FY 1972 to assist the States (1) to develop and improve public library service to persons without such service, (2) to provide library services for the handicapped, the institutionalized and the disadvantaged, both rural and urban, (3) to strengthen metropolitan public libraries, (4) to strengthen the capacity of the State Library Agency to meet the library and information needs of all the people, and (5) to develop systematic and effective coordination of the resources of all types of libraries. (LSCA titles I and III)

[2] General revenue sharing dollar amounts listed here include funds only promised as well as those actually received. Of these amounts, 97 percent come from local government revenue sharing entitlements and the remaining 3 percent from State entitlements. Libraries in many localities were advised that revenue sharing allotments this year were "one time only" funds. In several States, almost the entire revenue sharing amount shown above went to one library; for example, in Illinois, the Chicago Public Library received $1 million of the $1,262,614 allotted from local governments for library purposes.

American Library Association
Washington Office
Apr/May 1973

(Dollars in Thousands)

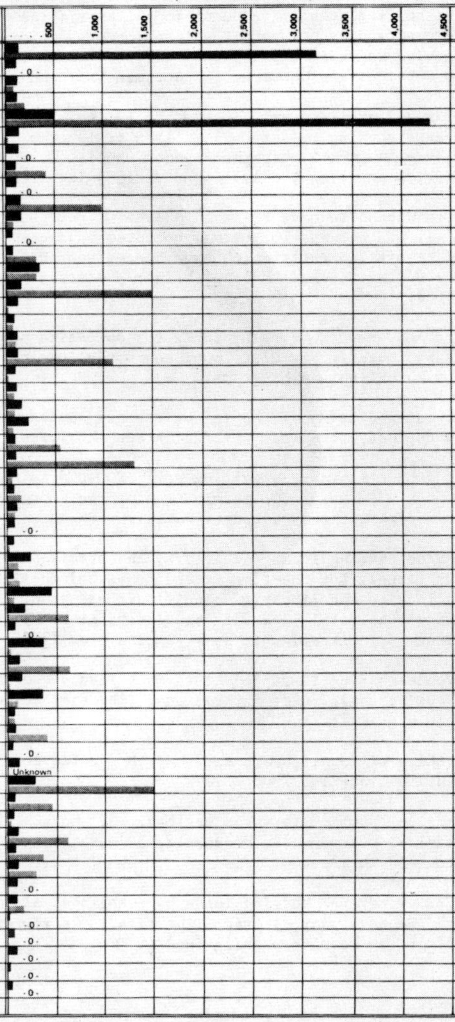

STATES	LSCA[1]	Revenue Sharing[2]
Alabama	170,495	3,284,233
Alaska	106,185	- 0 -
Arizona	136,279	127,250
Arkansas	139,366	250,000
California	508,399	4,342,987
Colorado	145,178	9,043
Connecticut	162,063	- 0 -
Delaware	111,219	404,706
District of Columbia	115,484	- 0 -
Florida	238,966	1,010,400
Georgia	193,939	106,000
Hawaii	115,759	- 0 -
Idaho	114,594	352,700
Illinois	327,480	316,933
Indiana	206,304	1,505,000
Iowa	157,823	10,000
Kansas	146,034	109,740
Kentucky	165,893	155,700
Louisiana	174,568	1,224,600
Maine	120,338	9,870
Maryland	180,283	126,000
Massachusetts	216,445	113,000
Michigan	281,654	75,000
Minnesota	177,882	597,500
Mississippi	145,376	1,371,291
Missouri	195,737	46,742
Montana	114,213	213,000
Nebraska	130,370	78,492
Nevada	110,003	- 0 -
New Hampshire	115,099	21,000
New Jersey	246,717	130,000
New Mexico	120,795	146,824
New York	472,327	92,497
North Carolina	204,019	621,700
North Dakota	112,644	- 0 -
Ohio	318,025	46,725
Oklahoma	152,383	742,135
Oregon	142,806	2,000
Pennsylvania	341,396	61,000
Rhode Island	119,439	87,300
South Carolina	153,022	447,000
South Dakota	113,637	- 0 -
Tennessee	180,319	Unknown
Texas	329,174	1,500,000
Utah	121,681	440,000
Vermont	109,103	19,000
Virginia	195,145	688,809
Washington	169,779	399,221
West Virginia	135,701	326,062
Wisconsin	190,426	- 0 -
Wyoming	106,804	153,790
American Samoa	20,568	- 0 -
Guam	21,779	- 0 -
Puerto Rico	155,510	- 0 -
Trust Territory	21,294	- 0 -
Virgin Islands	22,079	- 0 -
TOTALS	$9,500,000[1]	$21,765,250[2]

[1] LSCA grants to the States for construction of new public library buildings and the acquisition, expansion, remodeling, and alteration of existing buildings for use as public libraries, in accordance with the State plans for Statewide library development. (LSCA title II)

[2] General revenue sharing dollar amounts listed here include funds only promised as well as those actually received. Of these amounts, 92 percent come from local government revenue sharing entitlements and the remaining 8 percent from State entitlements for State library construction projects in two States. In several States, almost the entire revenue sharing amount shown above comes from one local governmental unit for one library construction project; for example, in Alabama, $3.2 million is for one library alone from one municipal governmental unit.

American Library Association
Washington Office
Apr/May 1973

<u>Public Libraries and General Revenue Sharing</u>
Comments from the State Library Agencies

<u>PENNSYLVANIA</u>   Local governments have tended to see the revenue sharing money as a
           means of holding down or reducing local taxes. The amount of money
going to individual governments does not permit allocation of sufficiently large sums
to inaugurate library service where none previously existed. Such demonstration grants
can be made with Library Services and Construction Act money if and when available.

<u>ILLINOIS</u>   Of the $1,579,547 promised or allocated to Illinois libraries from
           general revenue sharing to date, $1 million is for the Chicago Public
Library. In general, we are concerned that the revenue sharing is being used to reduce present local tax levies or to meet obligations already incurred.

<u>WISCONSIN</u>   Libraries in Wisconsin have received $365,800 from general revenue
           sharing. All of this was for normal operating budgets. If revenue
sharing is not continued, those libraries which have been given such money, will have
extreme difficulty making up the slack with local budget processes. Regression, not
progress, is the likelihood.

<u>NEW JERSEY</u>   It appears that revenue sharing funds for operating purposes are being
           used to substitute for regular local appropriations rather than to ex-
pand existing programs or establish new programs.

<u>TEXAS</u>   Other priority categories specified in the revenue sharing law are re-
           ceiving the funds, not libraries. Libraries are the lowest priority.

<u>MICHIGAN</u>   The Detroit Public Library is getting some $900,000 in general revenue
           sharing -- part to make up for termination of the Emergency Employment
Act, and part to make up for the library's budget cuts.

<u>OKLAHOMA</u>   General revenue sharing funds received by and promised libraries in
           Oklahoma are largely for one-time expenditures and the likelihood of
stable, recurring allocations to the libraries receiving these grants is slim. One
library received $203,000 of the total $282,835 actually received by Oklahoma
libraries; the balance went to 7 libraries in sums ranging from $700 to $17,500.

<u>NEW YORK</u>   Because revenue sharing is funded at so many levels and units of
           government, using these funds for regional libraries and cooperative
efforts is almost impossible.

<u>VIRGINIA</u>   Out of 134 units of local government, only 5 granted general revenue
           sharing funds to libraries.

<u>OHIO</u>   In Ohio there are 251 public library districts. Of these, 118 libraries
           wrote 345 proposals. Out of these proposals, 30 were funded amounting to
some $267,000 ranging from $50 to $36,000.

<u>CALIFORNIA</u>   To date county revenue sharing funds have not been allocated to the
           libraries. We have many district libraries in California, and these
have not been able to obtain any revenue sharing funds.

*   *   *

American Library Association
Washington Office
May, 1973

54

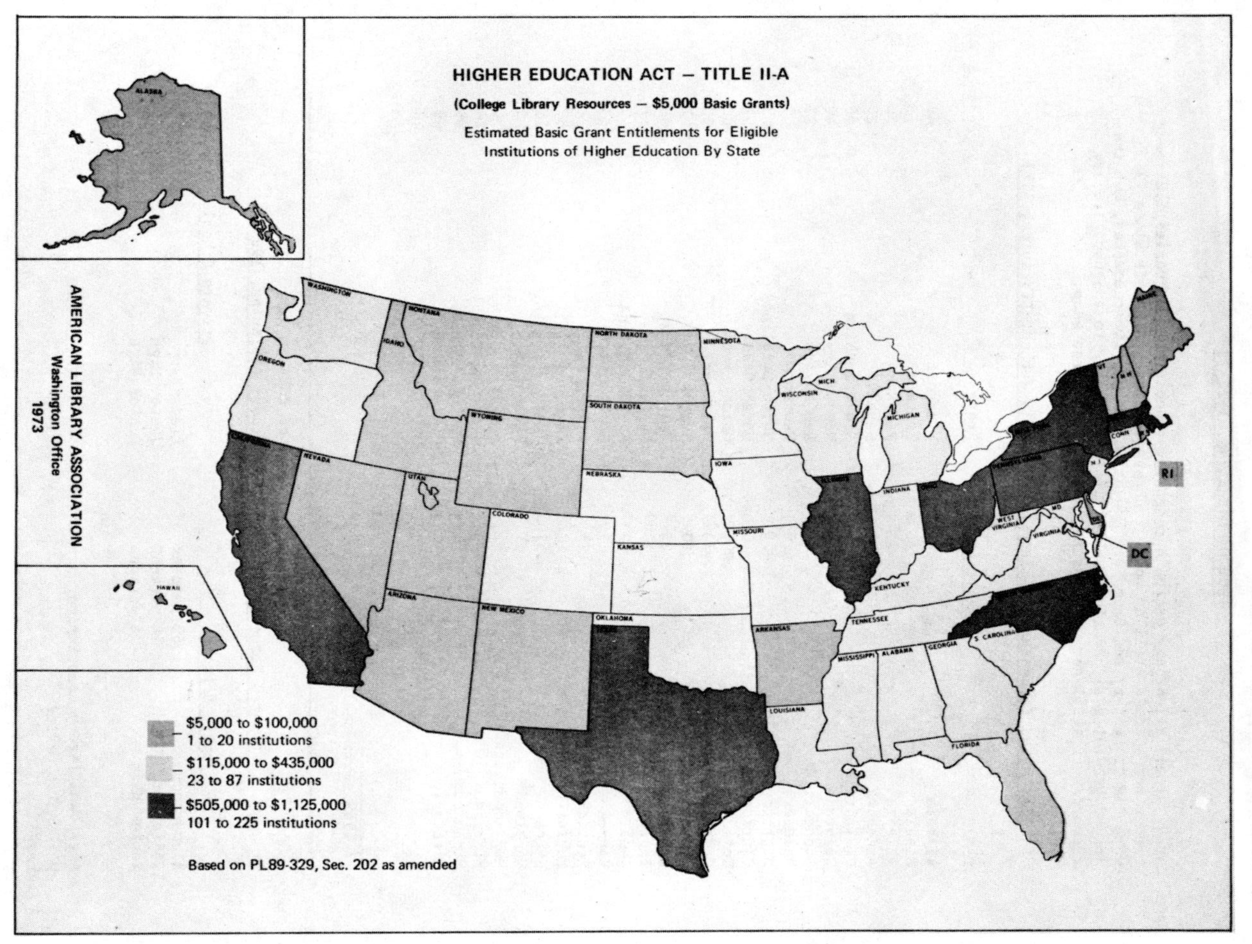

HIGHER EDUCATION ACT — TITLE II-A
(College Library Resources — $5,000 Basic Grants)
Estimated Basic Grant Entitlements for Eligible
Institutions of Higher Education By State
AMERICAN LIBRARY ASSOCIATION
Washington Office
1973
$5,000 to $100,000
1 to 20 institutions
$115,000 to $435,000
23 to 87 institutions
$505,000 to $1,125,000
101 to 225 institutions
Based on PL89-329, Sec. 202 as amended
ALASKA
HAWAII
RI
DC
WASHINGTON
OREGON
CALIFORNIA
NEVADA
IDAHO
MONTANA
WYOMING
UTAH
ARIZONA
NEW MEXICO
COLORADO
NORTH DAKOTA
SOUTH DAKOTA
NEBRASKA
KANSAS
OKLAHOMA
TEXAS
MINNESOTA
IOWA
MISSOURI
ARKANSAS
LOUISIANA
WISCONSIN
MICH
MICHIGAN
ILLINOIS
INDIANA
OHIO
KENTUCKY
TENNESSEE
MISSISSIPPI
ALABAMA
GEORGIA
FLORIDA
S. CAROLINA
VIRGINIA
WEST VIRGINIA
MD
PENNSYLVANIA
NEW YORK
VT
N. H.
CONN
N. J.
MAINE

Today almost all of the nation's secondary schools have libraries, but many
elementary schools still do not. Much progress has been made since 1965
when the Elementary and Secondary Education Act was first enacted, but the
job of providing all American school children access to adequate library
resources is still not done, as the following figures show:

Estimated Percentage of Elementary Schools Without Libraries, 1972

State	Percentage	State	Percentage
Alabama	5	Missouri	48
Alaska	60	Montana	75
Arizona	15	Nebraska	50
Arkansas	35	Nevada[1]	27
California	55	New Hampshire	66
Colorado	30	New Jersey	40
Connecticut	40	New Mexico	22
Delaware	0	New York	5
District of Columbia	0	North Carolina	3
Florida	0	North Dakota	51
Georgia	.001	Ohio	80
Hawaii	13	Oklahoma	68
Idaho	60	Oregon	7
Illinois	20	Pennsylvania	44
Indiana	20	Rhode Island	7
Iowa	40	South Carolina	3
Kansas	43	South Dakota	95
Kentucky	25	Tennessee	2
Louisiana	50	Texas	59
Maine	55	Utah	15
Maryland	11	Vermont	90
Massachusetts	35	Virginia	4
Michigan	30	Washington	20
Minnesota	.014	West Virginia[1]	95
Mississippi	40	Wisconsin	49
		Wyoming	48

---

[1] 1969 estimate latest available

Before Enactment of ESEA
Estimated Percentage of Schools Without Libraries, 1965

Public Schools		Private Schools	
Elementary	69 percent	Elementary	47 percent
Junior High	14 percent	Junior High	5 percent
Senior High	6 percent	Senior High	3 percent

American Library Association
Washington Office
May 1973

<u>Estimated Grants for School Library Resources--ESEA Title II</u>
(Note: totals include outlying territories not listed)

	1973 Appropriation[1]	1973 Allocation[2]	Decrease	1974 Budget
TOTALS....	$100,000,000	$90,000,000	$10,000,000	Zero
Alabama	1,576,446	1,418,801	157,645	-0-
Alaska	154,768	139,291	15,477	-0-
Arizona	880,504	792,454	88,050	-0-
Arkansas	899,666	809,699	89,967	-0-
California	9,555,979	8,600,381	955,598	-0-
Colorado	1,114,779	1,003,301	111,478	-0-
Connecticut	1,474,526	1,327,073	147,453	-0-
Delaware	284,778	256,300	28,478	-0-
Dist. of Col.	316,966	285,269	31,697	-0-
Florida	2,913,723	2,622,351	291,372	-0-
Georgia	2,138,801	1,924,921	213,880	-0-
Hawaii	395,231	355,708	39,523	-0-
Idaho	359,913	323,922	35,991	-0-
Illinois	5,372,023	4,834,821	537,202	-0-
Indiana	2,567,276	2,310,548	256,728	-0-
Iowa	1,409,424	1,268,482	140,942	-0-
Kansas	1,052,428	947,185	105,243	-0-
Kentucky	1,502,616	1,352,354	150,262	-0-
Louisiana	1,839,047	1,655,142	183,905	-0-
Maine	511,820	460,638	51,182	-0-
Maryland	1,976,418	1,778,776	197,642	-0-
Massachusetts	2,653,547	2,388,192	265,355	-0-
Michigan	4,607,269	4,146,542	460,727	-0-
Minnesota	1,989,124	1,790,212	198,912	-0-
Mississippi	1,051,644	946,480	105,164	-0-
Missouri	2,276,926	2,049,233	227,693	-0-
Montana	361,392	325,253	36,139	-0-
Nebraska	709,282	638,354	70,928	-0-
Nevada	251,573	226,416	25,157	-0-
New Hampshire	362,994	326,695	36,299	-0-
New Jersey	3,396,759	3,057,083	339,676	-0-
New Mexico	567,813	511,032	56,781	-0-
New York	8,159,503	7,343,552	815,951	-0-
North Carolina	2,299,340	2,069,406	229,934	-0-
North Dakota	305,974	275,377	30,597	-0-
Ohio	5,282,833	4,754,550	528,283	-0-
Oklahoma	1,212,516	1,091,264	121,252	-0-
Oregon	972,750	875,475	97,275	-0-
Pennsylvania	5,527,967	4,975,170	552,797	-0-
Rhode Island	441,064	396,958	44,106	-0-
South Carolina	1,250,369	1,125,332	125,037	-0-
South Dakota	339,742	305,768	33,974	-0-
Tennessee	1,772,102	1,594,892	177,210	-0-
Texas	5,596,863	5,037,176	559,687	-0-
Utah	584,952	526,457	58,495	-0-
Vermont	224,964	202,468	22,496	-0-
Virginia	2,154,844	1,939,360	215,484	-0-
Washington	1,650,100	1,485,090	165,010	-0-
West Virginia	783,532	705,179	78,353	-0-
Wisconsin	2,305,507	2,074,956	230,551	-0-
Wyoming	170,599	153,539	17,060	-0-

American Library Association
Washington Office
May, 1973

1/ Based on Congressional intent in HR 15417 passed and sent to White House August 10, 1972, and Continuing Resolution (PL 92-334, as amended).
2/ Based on President's FY 1973 Budget.

<u>The Need for Adequate Appropriations for ESEA Title II in FY 1974</u>
Based on 1973 reports from the States

<u>PENNSYLVANIA</u> Zero funding in FY 1974 of ESEA II would mean that new elementary school
libraries in many districts will not get past the planning stage where
they now are. Diocesan schools in the Commonwealth will be harmed, as new library
materials will be reduced to a trickle. Statewide, the removal of nearly $5 million
from our library materials budgets will result in cuts in acquisition of new library
material, loss of staff and use of facilities.

<u>KANSAS</u> While ESEA II has never been funded to meet expectations, the program has
served as a catalyst in Kansas to persuade reluctant school administrators
that good library media programs are of real value in securing needed educational
change. If ESEA II is discontinued in FY 1974, Kansas will lose 30 Right-to-Read projects. Kansas still needs over 200 elementary library media centers for schools of
over 150 students, and service from a qualified library media specialist for 377
schools of under 150 enrollment.

<u>MASSACHUSETTS</u> Despite great progress under ESEA II, even now over 1/3 of Massachu-
setts public schools still have no library media centers, and two-
thirds of those that do, still do not have a full-time professional staff person.
Since no state funds are available for development of school library media programs in
Massachusetts, the loss of ESEA II funds would mean that public and private schools
would be on their own to overcome serious program deficiencies in order to meet even
current, let alone future needs.

<u>OREGON</u> Zero-funding for ESEA II would mean nothing more than a severe financial blow
and a drastic adverse effect upon educational programs of Oregon's private
schools. A large portion of these have participated in this program. They look for-
ward annually to the use of new materials they would not possibly obtain otherwise.
Abrupt cut-off of ESEA II would cause great hardship to the education of Oregon's
public school children, too. Through this program, local schools have made a concer-
ted attempt to meet state standards.

<u>ARIZONA</u> Small schools in isolated areas of the state with budgets of less than $100
for library resources depend greatly on ESEA II minimum grants. Local level
support in many cases has been maintained only to qualify for ESEA II. If title II is
discontinued, local support will drop. ESEA II special grants have greatly assisted
Arizona's many new schools now opening each year in one of the fastest growing states
in the country.

<u>NEW YORK</u> The state is moving toward greater regionalization of educational services.
ESEA II has had a direct role in the development of regional school library
media centers and services. Such centers are designed to provide resources and services which supplement local programs. The loss of ESEA II would severely curtail regional efforts which provide badly-needed services and resources in an efficient and
economical manner.

<u>ILLINOIS</u> The termination of ESEA II program would have far-reaching effects at all
levels of media service. Instructional materials collections available to
individual children will be fewer in number and more narrow in scope. Funds will not
be available for the development of district or cooperative instructional materials
centers. Consultative services will no longer be available from the Office of the
Superintendent of Public Instruction to aid in the development of all types of media
services at all levels. In some cases, the withdrawal of ESEA II funds will mean the
loss of up to 50 percent of a school district's total instructional materials budget.

*　　　　　*　　　　　*

American Library Association
Washington Office
May, 1973

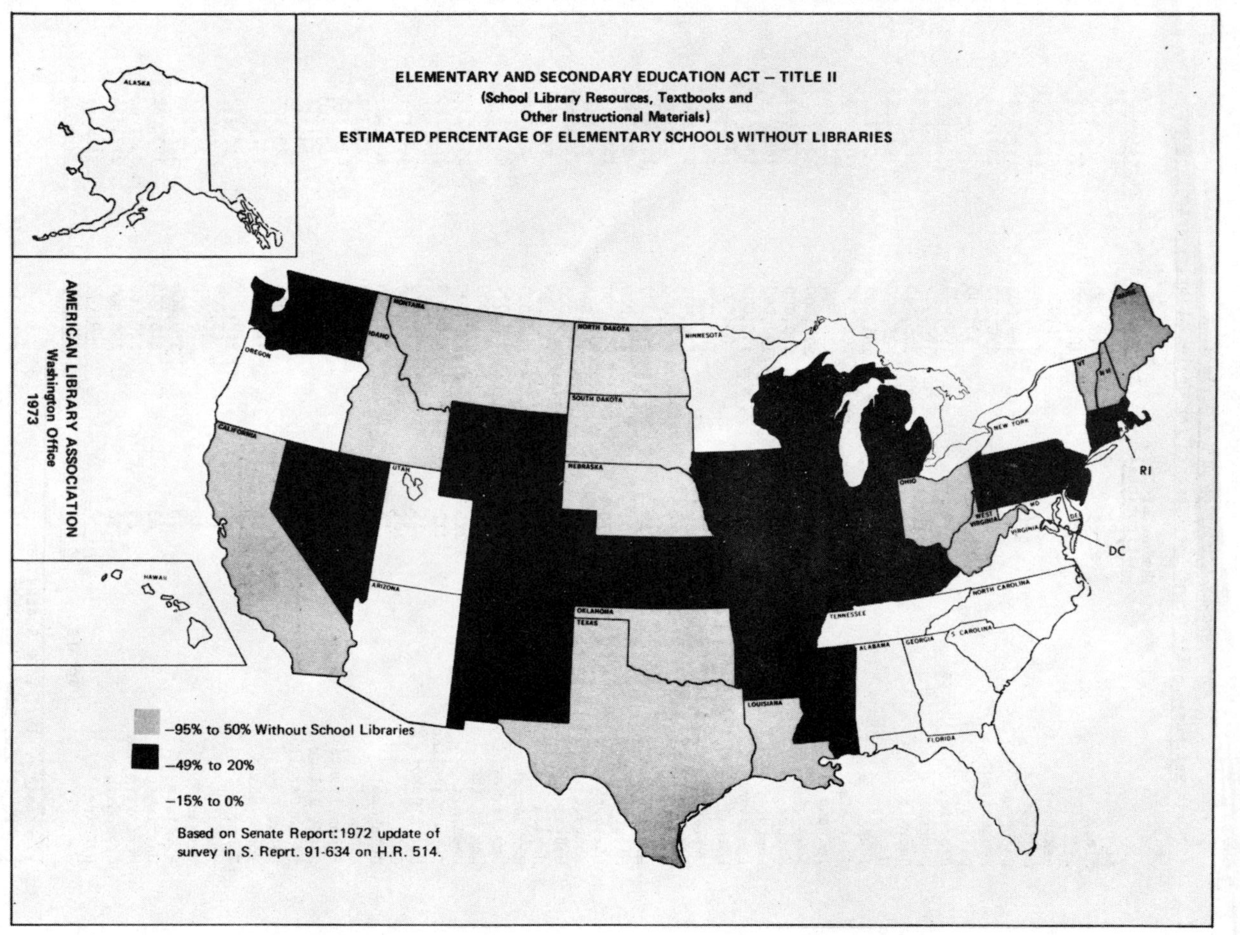

ELEMENTARY AND SECONDARY EDUCATION ACT — TITLE II
(School Library Resources, Textbooks and
Other Instructional Materials)
ESTIMATED PERCENTAGE OF ELEMENTARY SCHOOLS WITHOUT LIBRARIES
ALASKA
HAWAII
AMERICAN LIBRARY ASSOCIATION
Washington Office
1973
—95% to 50% Without School Libraries
—49% to 20%
—15% to 0%
Based on Senate Report:1972 update of
survey in S. Reprt. 91-634 on H.R. 514.

<u>HIGHER EDUCATION ACT - Title II-A</u>
<u>Estimated Basic Grant Entitlements for College Library Resources</u>

	Number of Institutions [1]	Maximum Entitlement [2]	Enrollment [1]
Alabama	51	$255,000	110,435
Alaska	3	15,000	11,630
Arizona	20	100,000	123,722
Arkansas	19	95,000	53,850
California	217	1,085,000	1,310,758
Colorado	32	160,000	127,842
Connecticut	46	230,000	130,960
Delaware	7	35,000	28,248
District of Columbia	20	100,000	80,565
Florida	64	320,000	255,916
Georgia	61	305,000	140,743
Hawaii	13	65,000	42,418
Idaho	9	45,000	34,536
Illinois	138	690,000	483,195
Indiana	44	220,000	201,424
Iowa	54	270,000	109,454
Kansas	52	260,000	107,973
Kentucky	36	180,000	108,047
Louisiana	23	115,000	134,409
Maine	17	85,000	34,551
Maryland	48	240,000	**167**,773
Massachusetts	118	**590**,000	**319,856**
Michigan	87	435,000	407,338
Minnesota	59	295,000	157,291
Mississippi	41	205,000	80,265
Missouri	70	350,000	188,001
Montana	12	60,000	28,081
Nebraska	27	135,000	66,054
Nevada	6	30,000	17,271
New Hampshire	19	95,000	28,294
New Jersey	58	290,000	241,189
New Mexico	11	55,000	47,953
New York	225	1,125,000	851,273
North Carolina	113	565,000	193,389
North Dakota	12	60,000	29,765
Ohio	101	505,000	385,581
Oklahoma	40	200,000	121,927
Oregon	40	200,000	123,322
Pennsylvania	146	730,000	429,838
Rhode Island	13	65,000	49,320
South Carolina	46	230,000	93,771
South Dakota	16	80,000	28,909
Tennessee	62	310,000	147,299
Texas	134	670,000	487,028
Utah	13	65,000	82,277
Vermont	18	90,000	25,712
Virginia	70	350,000	177,089
Washington	43	215,000	192,062
West Virginia	24	120,000	64,665
Wisconsin	58	290,000	217,114
Wyoming	8	40,000	17,551
TOTALS	2,664	$13,320,000	9,106,885

[1] Based on 1972 USOE Statistics
[2] PL 92-318, Education Amdts. of 1972, mandates a matching basic grant of up to $5,000 for every eligible institution of higher education.

<u>Library Training</u>
<u>The Need for Adequate Appropriations for HEA II-B Fellowships and Traineeships</u>

Comments from deans and department heads in the field of library & information science

<u>MICHIGAN, Wayne State University Department of Library Science</u>
Nationwide and for all types of libraries, the urgent need is for librarians representing minority and disadvantaged groups to work with urban and rural poor and to give all
libraries larger numbers of minority librarians who will relate effectively with
minority clientele. Many qualified applicants cannot afford the rising costs of
graduate education.

<u>CALIFORNIA, UCLA Graduate School of Library Service</u>
Rising costs (tuition, fees, books, supplies, living) and diminishing institutional
financial aid are excluding qualified candidates for admission, particularly those of
minority ethnic backgrounds who are generally in the least favorable financial position. State support is inadequate to meet increasing costs; in some cases state
support has actually decreased.

<u>GEORGIA, Atlanta University School of Library Service</u>
Continuing education programs are most vital to keep librarians abreast of new
developments in the profession. Library schools need federal support to continue
such programs. There continue to be a shortage of library school teachers at the
graduate and undergraduate levels. The HEA II-B program has done much to alleviate
this situation; however, there is a great need for this program to continue not only
for the preparation of teachers, but also for the education of subject and technical
specialists and administrators.

<u>INDIANA, Indiana University Graduate Library School</u>
Financial aid at the master's degree level makes it possible for librarianship to
compete for recruits (1) who have outstanding qualifications, (2) who have sound
science and foreign language competencies, and (3) who come from disadvantaged backgrounds. These are the people we need most in today's libraries and who probably
won't come to library school without financial support.

<u>MICHIGAN, University of Michigan School of Library Science</u>
In 1971-72, 52 percent of the students admitted to our master's degree program in
library science were unable to attend the University of Michigan; in almost every
instance their inability to come was due to financial problems.

<u>MINNESOTA, University of Minnesota Library School</u>
Library education has been severely handicapped by the unavailability of fellowship
funds, whereas anatomy and anthropology, physics, and many other fields do not expect
to recruit any graduate student without a healthy stipend, library schools have had
no stipends, before 1966 and after 1971.

<u>NEW JERSEY, Rutgers Graduate School of Library Service</u>
All of the great talk about giving educational opportunities to disadvantaged persons
will be to no avail if individuals cannot, in fact, afford to attend professional
schools. With tuition and living costs rising, fellowships are more needed now than
ever before.

<u>MASSACHUSETTS, Simmons College School of Library Science</u>
Since librarianship tends to attract students from moderate income families, or
young people who have families of their own, many fine candidates are prevented from
entering librarianship for lack of funds. Of the approximately 1,200 applications for
admission we receive each year, 95 percent request and require financial aid, which
we presently cannot offer.

*   *   *

American Library Association
Washington Office
May, 1973

61

Ms. Cooke. Our concern includes libraries of all kinds, and their prospects have never been as imperiled in all the years in which we have been privileged to appear before this subcommittee as they are this year.

In looking at the 1974 budget, we find that there are no funds authorized for any of the major library programs—the Library Services and Construction Act, Title II of the Elementary and Secondary Education Act, nor Title II of the Higher Education Act.

The American Library Association firmly believes that all these programs have been highly successful in stimulating State and local support and that their continuation is essential if further library development is to be realized. In fact, the full authorizations reflect the real needs if these library programs are to fulfill their vital roles in undergirding the entire gamut of educational activities.

However, considering the budgetary constraints under which the subcommittee is operating, we are recommending for the most part that you provide the same amounts Congress approved last year in the vetoed bill, H.R. 15417. [See attached table of funds for library-related programs.]

We also urge that the subcommittee give prompt, favorable consideration to approval of a separate education appropriation bill, as you did in fiscal years 1971 and 1972. As you know, the delay in funding education programs and the uncertainty that accompanies operation under a continuing resolution work many hardships on programs and personnel alike. In fiscal year 1974, a continuing resolution unless carefully worded to include specific dollar amounts for individual library programs will result in their abrupt termination based on the President's budget.

A matter of increasing concern to the association now is the information that we are beginning to receive from the States regarding the mounting crisis for library personnel. Over 2,300 library employees will have to be laid off in the new fiscal year beginning July 1. People have been given termination notices. The same situation applies at the Federal level. These people cannot be kept dangling awaiting final action on an HEW appropriation bill. Some have vacation time accrued and are starting to look for other jobs right now. Up until now the administration has placed low priority on books and buildings, but now it is jobs and people that are at stake. Frankly, we are very much concerned. In addition to proposing that the subcommittee maintain funding for library programs in fiscal year 1974 at the level of the vetoed bill, H.R. 15417, we are strongly urging that the legislative history of the 1974 Appropriation Act make clear that there is a mandatory expenditure requirement under section 415 of the General Education Provisions Act (Public Law 230, as amended).

Currently operating under a rather ambiguous continuing resolution, the Secretary of HEW, Mr. Weinberger, has apparently decided to view the measure as a discretionary authority establishing simply a maximum or outer spending limit and not a fixed or mandatory one. Consequently, some library programs that were already underway in 1973 are having to be curtailed.

We had hoped earlier in the year there might be a regular 1973 appropriation bill. Now, belatedly, some of these programs are being cut back. For the library programs under the Library Services and Construction Act, we are recommending $84.5 million. That is the level that you approved in H.R. 15417. That would provide $62 million for services, $15 million more construction, and $7.5 million for Interlibrary Cooperation. In that connection, we have attached allotment tables to show you the variations between what the current spending level is being interpreted under the continuing resolution and what in fact the committee or the Congress had approved in the vetoed bill.

Come July 1, under such a continuing resolution there would be abrupt termination of many library programs. I realize that, at least I hope, no library would close down, but there are special projects that would close down. In many cases it is programs for the disadvantaged and for the blind and handicapped. This is the one that supplements the Library of Congress materials that are sent out to the States and regions.

We urge that specific dollar amounts be mentioned in the bill if another continuing resolution is essential.

With regard to revenue sharing, we have also attached some charts for your perusal. You will find them quite fascinating. We have some descriptive comments from the States, their reactions to it. On the first glance the charts show that the outlook seems quite promising for library programs, but there are many questions that are unanswered. For example, we found in many cases the funds are merely anticipated. They have not actually been received.

In other cases, the libraries have been warned, "This is a one-time thing; don't expect it again. You have had your chance." Given the uncertainty of general revenue sharing at this time and the fact the legislative history has made clear it is not intended to replace categorical aid, we again would recommend that you provide an adequate appropriation to continue the Library Services and Construction Act.

We submit that the LSCA programs that we have described in here as exemplary reflect sound and creative use of the support provided under all three titles and also proof of the wisdom of the decision of Congress to continue this program through fiscal year 1976, when it was amended and extended in 1970 (Public Law 91–600). The 1970 amendments have given the States even greater discretion in deciding how the funds are to be used, and we feel that this program as well as Title II under the Elementary and Secondary Education Act does indeed reflect the philosophy of the administration in returning power to the people because the decisions as to how the funds are to be spent are indeed made by the people, for the most part through the broadly representative advisory councils established.

In contrast with title III of the Library Services and Construction Act, the interlibrary cooperation title, we feel that revenue sharing is totally unsuitable because it is directed at specific cities and towns. It has no counterpart for cooperation. In fact, it may indeed have the opposite effect by forcing the localities to be concerned strictly with their own concerns rather than broader intergovernmental kind of sharing.

Turning to school libraries under title II of the Elementary and Secondary Education Act, we recommend appropriation of $100 million, which would maintain this program at the level approved in H.R. 15417. This program is another candidate for extinction under the budget proposal to zero it out.

The States report that on an average nearly one-third of their elementary schools still lack libraries, and the Office of Education reported in 1970 that no more than half of the secondary schools in any State met their own State standards for school libraries.

Attached to the statement is a map and comments reflecting some of the accomplishments in the States and the fact that we still have quite a way to go.

Mr. FLOOD. Thank you. Those exhibits look good.

Ms. COOKE. Thank you very much.

As you know, we are also concerned with title II of the Higher Education Act, we recommend a $30 million appropriation and we have a map showing the entitlements estimated there with the institution figures plus some comments on library training and demonstration needs.

Mr. FLOOD. Thank you.

Ms. COOKE. Thank you very much for this opportunity.

———

THE CRISIS IN OUR NATIONAL LIBRARY SYSTEM:
A Statement by a Group of Concerned Citizens

The undersigned individuals are convinced that it would be seriously detrimental to the public interest and produce long-range adverse effects on American society to reverse, as proposed in the Federal Executive Budget, the established national policy in support of an organized and coordinated system of library services in the United States. That established policy is clearly set forth in the following provision of Public Law 91-345, The National Commission on Libraries and Information Science Act of 1970:

> "<u>The Congress hereby affirms that library and information services adequate to meet the needs of the people of the United States are essential to achieve national goals and to utilize most effectively the Nation's educational resources and that the Federal Government will cooperate with state and local governments and public and private agencies in assuming optimum provision of such services.</u>"

President Nixon on July 20, 1970, signed these words into law as a carefully considered statement of enduring national policy. It was a policy supported by both political parties, by both houses of Congress, and the Executive Branch during both

-more-

the Johnson and Nixon administrations.

This law recognized a profound national interest in adequate library services, a national interest greater than the sum
of the interests of individual States, communities, and institutions. Implicit in the law is the recognition of many aspects
of that national interest:

> That bringing educational opportunity
> to children, particularly disadvantaged chil-
> dren so that they can break through barriers
> of poverty and discrimination, requires
> school libraries with an abundant choice of
> reading and special instructional materials;

> That not only students and faculty but
> the whole nation gains from the strength of
> the learning and research resources of col-
> lege and university libraries;

> That each of our great research collec-
> tions is a _national_ resource deserving na-
> tional support;

> That only through our library systems
> can most Americans have meaningful access to
> the enormous intellectual and information
> resources embodied in the tens of thousands

-more-

of books annually published and the hundreds

of thousands from prior years that are ac-

tively in use;

And finally, that only through a nation-

ally conceived system can all of our librar-

ies be linked to serve our national needs

efficiently and economically.

This statement of policy gave a capstone of unity to pro-

visions already existing in separate laws. The Library Ser-

vices and Construction Act makes funds available on a matching

basis to improve public library services and extend them to un-

served areas and groups. The National Defense Education Act

provides for school library collections in special areas of na-

tional interest and gives aid in acquiring films, language

tapes, and other special materials. It also assists in the de-

velopment of research collections in designated university cen-

ters. The Elementary and Secondary Education Act provides

funds to establish and maintain school libraries serving chil-

dren, many of whom in poor urban and rural districts had never

had a school library. The Higher Education Act provides as-

sistance to college and university libraries and for central

cataloging and bibliographical services performed by the Li-

brary of Congress. And finally, Public Law 91-345 which contains

the statement of policy quoted above as its preamble, established

-more-

67

a National-Commission on Libraries and Information Science to
plan and make recommendations for the implementation of the
policy.

The Executive Budget submitted to Congress for the Fiscal
Year beginning July 1, 1973, abandons completely this firmly
established national policy. Act by act, title by title, it
eliminates every single penny of support for libraries (other
than those of the Federal Government itself). Gone would be
library funds under the National Defense Education Act, the Library Services and Construction Act, the Elementary and Secondary Education Act, and the Higher Education Act. Added injury
would result from a sharp increase in postal rates, raising the
cost of books and magazines to every buyer, including libraries.

The impact of this sudden and devastating reversal of national policy will extend far beyond the institutions immediately damaged. Federal funds provide only a small portion of
the total support of libraries. Basic costs of buildings and
salaries are met primarily from local, State and institutional
funds. But Federal funds have provided the stimulation and the
means for <u>extended</u> services, for <u>new</u> ventures, for <u>coordina-
tion</u> of activities, for <u>enriched</u> programs and <u>innovative</u> materials. Federal funds have brought library services to remote

-more-

68

farms by bookmobile. They have brought school libraries into
urban slums, and new branches of public libraries into the sub-
urbs. They have created a market that has made it possible to
publish and to bring to inner-city children books reflecting
their experiences and responding to their needs. It has been
Federal funds that have enabled school libraries to acquire new
instructional materials in all media. Federal funding has made
it possible to create and use new kinds of vocational teaching
materials for young men and women with limited reading skill.
It is Federal funding, too, that has helped to create the libraries of our hundreds of new community colleges and technical
institutes. At the same time Federal appropriations have
helped to import and catalog foreign publications to strengthen
the advanced research collections needed by our universities
and scholars. Federal funds have helped to encourage the development of statewide systems linking libraries together within each State. Federal funds are just beginning to provide the
basis for a nationally linked system.

Federal funding has often provided the stimulus and the
leadership for the development of new kinds of library materials and for the offering of new services, and for the extension
of existing library services to people who never before enjoyed
them. It is these critically needed and innovative services of

-more-

libraries that would be strangled by the sudden and total withdrawal of funds as proposed in the Executive Budget. The suf-
ferers would be the children of the great cities and the rural
areas, the young men and women seeking job training in technical institutes, the adults seeking information beyond the current flow of news, the researchers needing special materials
and advanced information systems. The ultimate sufferer would
be the national interest.

Revenue sharing has been proposed as an answer, but it is
not. Needs that are primarily local or institutional will and
should be met with local or institutional funds, whether they
come from local taxes or from revenue sharing. But in the
words of the law "library and information services adequate to
meet the needs of the people of the United States are essential to meet national goals." The national interest cannot be
allowed to rest on scattered, parochial and unpredictable local
actions. Without a sound national policy we could never have
created a national broadcasting system or a national telephone
system. The same is true for an effective national library
system.

Because the present assault on library funding is contained in so many different bills and titles and affects so
many kinds of institutions, its total impact has been hard to

-more-

grasp. The public does not fully realize what a crisis we
face. The signers of this statement believe a full public un-
derstanding of this emergency is urgently needed. The House of
Representatives took one essential and statesman-like step on
June 26, 1973, when it included funds for continuing the Federal library programs in the H.E.W. Appropriations Bill for fiscal 1974. But this is only one of the many actions which are
needed to resolve the issues both for the immediate future and
the long run.

We urge the Congress, through an appropriate committee or
committees, to call early public hearings to analyse the total
impact of this proposed reversal of Federal policy.

We urge the National Commission on Libraries and Information Science, charged by law with advising "the President and
the Congress on the implementation of national policy by such
statements, presentations, and reports as it deems appropriate," to act immediately to advise the President and the Congress of the aggregate effects of the Executive Budget on the
implementation of national library and information science policy.

We urge all associations, institutions, and citizens concerned with the free and adequate flow of information and
knowledge in the United States to give immediate and concerned

-more-

attention to the present crisis.

And finally, we urge the National Book Committee, in cooperation with other organizations, to initiate and carry
through with such action as may be necessary to create a full
public awareness of the scope and severity of the problems we
confront.

The following individuals, whose affiliation is given
for identification purposes only, have endorsed
the preceding statement

Morris B. Abram
Paul, Weiss, Goldberg, Rifkind
   Garrison and Wharton

Douglass Cater, President
Communications & Society Program
   Joint Program of Aspen
    Institute for Humanistic
    Studies and Academy for
    Educational Development

Walter Curley, Director
Cleveland Public Library

Richard Darling, Dean
Graduate School of Library
   Service
Columbia University

William S. Dix
University Librarian
Princeton University

Arnold W. Ehrlich
Editor-in-Chief
Publishers Weekly

Eli Evans
Carnegie Corporation of New York

Stephen M. Fischer
Assistant to the Publisher
Scientific American

Congressman William D. Ford

Charles Frankel
Old Dominion Professor of
   Philosophy and Public
   Affairs
Columbia University

John C. Frantz, Executive
   Chairman
National Book Committee

Robert W. Frase
Consulting Economist

Samuel B. Gould
Commission on Non-traditional
   Study

Francis Keppel, Chairman
General Learning Corporation

Dan Lacy, Senior Vice
   President
McGraw-Hill, Inc.

-more-

Jean E. Lowrie, Dean
School of Librarianship
Western Michigan University

Kenneth D. McCormick, Senior
    Editorial Consultant
Doubleday Publishing Company

Herbert Mitgang, President
Authors Guild

Foster Mohrhardt
Senior Program Officer
Council on Library Resources

Carol Nemeyer, Senior Associate
Association of American
    Publishers

Elnora M. Portteus, President
American Association of
    School Librarians
    (1972-73)
Supervisor of School Libraries
Cleveland Public Schools

M. J. Rossant, Director
The Twentieth Century Fund

Ross B. Sackett, President
Encyclopaedia Britannica
Educational Corporation

John Sessions
Assistant Director of Education
AFL/CIO

Roger L. Stevens, Chairman
National Book Committee

Arthur B. Tourtellot, President
CBS Foundation

Theodore Waller, President
Grolier Educational Corporation

Howard R. Webber, Director
The M.I.T. Press

Robert Wedgeworth, Executive
    Director
American Library Association

# # #

RESOLUTION TO U.S. CONGRESS

WHEREAS President Nixon proposed to end major grants-in-aid to libraries in FY 1974; and

WHEREAS this annihilation of needed and effective programs would result in devastating reduction or elimination of services to millions of library users; and

WHEREAS public libraries in every state, public and private school libraries in every congressional district, and the nation's college, university, and academic research libraries would suffer loss of urgently needed funds at a time when most libraries are already experiencing financial difficulty; and

WHEREAS the President twice vetoed the appropriations for the Departments of Labor and Health, Education, and Welfare in FY 1973, and as a result federally supported library programs are now entering the 8th month of the fiscal year with great uncertainty and, in some cases, at near crisis level of reduced funds; and

WHEREAS the President now proposed to impound or rescind almost $3 million of FY 1973 funds for college library resources for training, fellowships and the support for library education, and for research and demonstration programs authorized under title II of the Higher Education Act, despite the fact that on October 31 he signed this appropriation into law; and

WHEREAS by all these actions the President has shown that he claims the right to dictate educational priorities for the nation, contrary to the mandate of Congress; now therefore be it

RESOLVED that the American Library Association expresses its grave concern over these erosions of the constitutional powers of Congress in the determination of national priorities, and urges the Congress (1) to move quickly to enact a third Labor-HEW appropriations bill for FY 1973 and override another veto should that occur; and (2) to enact a FY 1974 appropriation for libraries to meet the needs of all the people whose access to information is the key to effective participation and often the key to survival itself.

Adopted by Council, American Library Association
January 30, 1973

The Association of American University Presses, Inc.

One Park Avenue, New York, N.Y. 10016 · 212 889-6040

<u>Memorandum of Resolution</u>

The Board of Directors of the Association of American University Presses,
on behalf of its United States members, voted at its 1973 Annual Meeting
in Austin, Texas, to express publicly to the National Book Committee its
deep concern with the FY 1974 U.S. budget that proposes, as submitted, to
terminate Federal support for library programs authorized under the
Library Services and Construction Act, under Title II of the Elementary
and Secondary Education Act, and under Title II of the Higher Education
Act (with the exception of the Library of Congress program authorized
under Part C of Title II). The Association represents U.S. university
presses located throughout the country. Among them, they publish in book
and other form works of scholarly and cultural importance produced at or
associated with principal institutions of higher education in North America.

In the judgment of the Board, the proposed Federal budget, if funded and
implemented in its present form will have effects--direct and indirect--
tending to interrupt the free flow of books upon which learning at many
levels depends. Appropriate responses to national challenges, in the
view of the Board, rely on an unimpeded dissemination of information,
and it gravely notes that elements of the proposed Federal budget that
restrict library services of several kinds do not appear to be compensated
for by revenue-sharing on non-Federal levels. That budget is therefore
likely to reduce the capacity of American learning to make those vital
responses and the capacity of the American people to act upon them.

June 19, 1973

Date Due

**DO NOT REMOVE
CARD FROM POCKET**

 PRINTED IN U.S.A.